BLUE TRAIL BREAKTHROUGH

Forging High-Performing Teams
in Unexpected Places

Bob Berk, PhD and Ari Berk

A leadership fable set
in a completely fictional camp

TERN TABLE
PRESS

BLUE TRAIL BREAKTHROUGH

Print edition ISBN 979-8-9917107-0-1
eBook edition ISBN 979-8-9917107-1-8

Published by Tern Table Press.
Book Design by David Maxine.
Front Cover Design by Pankaj Singh Renu.

TERN TABLE
P R E S S

newtableconsulting.com
bluetrailbreakthrough.com

PART I

THE STORY

CHAPTER 1

GOODBYE, STARRY SKY

ROBYN was the last one to sign. Maria stared at her loopy signature after Robyn picked up the pen, searching within herself for the sense of accomplishment and excitement that she knew she should be feeling. Instead, she found nerves and a not-insignificant measure of guilt.

"I know I've said it a million times, and I'll probably say it a million more times, but thank you," Maria said.

Lane smiled. "We wouldn't do it if we didn't believe in you, 100 percent."

They were sitting at Robyn and Lane's kitchen table in their house in Tucson. This house, which was also Robyn and Lane's winter office, was one of Maria's favorite places. There were huge windows looking out onto the Santa Catalina mountains. The sun was setting, flattering every rock face with its orange glow.

After they they finished with the signing, the three of them would go out for a celebratory dinner at Robyn and Lane's favorite grill.

"We're just happy that you'll have the opportunity you deserve. Even if it's not at Starry Sky," Robin said. "You've given so much to us over the years, and — "

"I understand," Maria interrupted. "Camps are family businesses."

"But you are family, Maria," Lane said. "I mean, every summer since you were eight years old, we've seen you running around, growing, leading people."

"Leading? When I was eight?"

"Leading, ordering around, whatever your cabin mates wanted to call it at the time," Robyn said. "But it's been such a joy to see you grow from that mighty little camper, with that water bottle almost as big as you were, all the way to now, about to be running the show at a camp of your very own."

But it won't be Starry Sky, moaned the bitter internal voice that had been hounding Maria for months, ever since Robyn and Lane had told her she wouldn't be taking over the camp where she grew up.

Maria had meant what she said. Many camps were indeed family businesses, and she'd known this since she was old enough to understand that camp was not only a magical summer wonderland, but a whole operation, complete with job descriptions, payroll, hirings and firings. Lane had inherited Camp Starry Sky from his father, and Lane's father from his father. When Lane married Robyn, she'd been given a director position as well. Once Lane and Robyn's daughter, Kelly, had become a counselor, it was impossible not to hear people's constant jokes about the inevitability of her ascending to the "throne." There were even a few jokes about her usurping Maria's position as the "heir."

Maria tuned them out. Kelly was smart and compassionate and capable and had obviously grown up living and breathing Starry Sky, even more so than Maria. They had a good relationship, and Starry Sky would be in great hands if Kelly was the one to take over. But by the time Kelly became a counselor in training, or a CIT, as they are known, Maria was in her second summer of being a senior counselor. When Kelly made it to senior counselor, Maria was promoted to assistant director. She'd allowed herself to hope, just a little, that Robyn and Lane might break tradition.

They'd broken the news in the nicest way possible, keeping it kind and short, just like they'd taught her to do when firing someone.

"Kelly told us last week that she's interested in becoming a co-director for a few years after she graduates college to see if she wants to spend her career in the camping world. Nothing's for sure, but it's seeming more likely that she'll eventually want to buy the camp from us and run it. More than you could ever know, we appreciate everything you've given to Starry Sky. And we'd love to support you in achieving your dream of running your own camp."

But this was twelve weeks ago—a summer and a half, in camp time. Now, Maria smiled with total authenticity and told her mentors, "I'm so grateful you all have given me this chance."

"It's not charity," Lane said. "We're expecting to see a return on our investment!"

His tone was light, and Maria knew he was trying to express confidence, but the nerves in her gut waxed once again, and her excitement waned a little more. Robyn and Lane had facilitated basically the entire process of purchasing Camp Blue Trail. Before the camp had officially gone on the market, they'd heard rumors about it from a friend of a friend of Blue Trail's director. Delicately, they'd reached out to Blue Trail's director and told him about Maria. She didn't know precisely what Robyn and Lane said about her, and she would've loved to be a fly on the wall for that phone conversation, but whatever they'd said had been good enough for the director to want to meet Maria and agree to sell her the camp shortly thereafter. Finally, Robyn and Lane had even co-signed the bank loan she'd used to purchase Camp Blue

Trail. They'd offered to do so right after telling her about Kelly's decision.

The stressful part, however, was that they had collateralized the purchase with their equity in their own camp. If Maria couldn't get Blue Trail back on track, there was the potential that they would have to sell Starry Sky. Ultimately, this was how Maria knew that Robyn and Lane really believed in her. It would have been an awful risk to take if they didn't.

To Maria, it still felt like an awful risk, but she tried to project confidence.

"You will see a return," she said. "It's a good camp, it doesn't have any trouble recruiting, the culture just needs some tweaking, I really believe that."

"There's no such thing as a culture tweak," Robyn said. "Especially at a camp. Camps are all culture. I mean, remember how long it took us to agree on new cabin names? Culture doesn't exist in a vacuum, everyone who's there plays a part in creating it. If the person at the top doesn't have a clear vision for what that culture should be and doesn't actively try to uphold it every day, it reverts to the default; whatever 'the way things have always been' is. And right now, despite their sterling reputation, Blue Trail's culture is hurting its enrollment. You're going to have to figure out why that is and how to change it."

See discussion activity 1.1 at the end of the chapter

"Every year they come to the American Camp Association Conference and talk about how beautiful it is on their lake, and how they just bought some new toys that also happen to go perfectly with their old traditions," Lane said. "And that may work for recruiting—obviously we have our own bias, but if Starry Sky didn't exist, we might have sent Kelly to Blue Trail. But Robyn's right. Camps need to be almost full to make enough money to weather any downturns, not to mention for you to take the kind of salary you need to support yourself the whole year."

Maria knew all this, of course. Recruitment at Blue Trail may have been fine, but years of being unable to retain campers for multi-summer tenures had finally led to a 25 percent drop in enrollment at Blue Trail from a decade ago. On the plus side, a camp that would have ordinarily been far too expensive for Maria was now available at a generous discount. The owner was clearly ready to be out of the camping business and had no delusions about inflating the price of his camp, based on its history alone.

On the other hand, Maria had much work to do to bring the camp back to where it needed to be. And if she couldn't do it, Robyn and Lane might lose the camp they'd spent their lives building.

"We were in a similar place when we took over Starry Sky from Lane's parents, though," Robyn said. "And now we have some of the best retention rates in the country."

"And we're proud of it," Lane added. "But yeah, that was no tweak or accident. We had a unified vision for how we wanted camp to be run, from the activities all the way up to the administrative culture. And, most importantly, we found the right people to help us get there. You were one of those people." He smiled at her. "Which is why we have the utmost confidence that you're the person Blue Trail needs. But, as you know, it's not easy finding the right people to turn your vision into a reality and it often takes multiple tries."

See discussion activity 1.2 at the end of the chapter

Maria had met three of the four other members of Blue Trail's leadership team when she'd flown out to see the camp a while back. She liked them. There was Stu, the parent liaison, who'd dropped out of the corporate world to work at Blue Trail nineteen years ago, and bragged that he hadn't fully shaved his long gray beard since; Jamie, the assistant director who had even answered Maria's most obscure, finely-detailed questions about Blue Trail operations and lore; and Laverne, the sardonic activities director who Maria guessed would be a good counterweight to Jamie's exuberance. She'd also spoken on the phone with Nico, their trips director, who was in his last year of college. But it was one thing to seem like a good person to work with when showing the new director around camp. Maria herself had conducted extremely promising interviews with several counselors and staff members who ended up not being invited back for another summer at Starry Sky.

As if reading her thoughts, Robyn spoke up.

"In part, your first summer will be about figuring out who gets to stay, who gets to be a part of this new Blue Trail you're creating," she said. "The best advice we can give you is to take the time to observe. Spend the first summer learning everything you can about how the camp operated without you. That doesn't mean don't do your job or be active as a director. But, allow people to show you who they are and who they can be on a collaborative team, so you can use this information to choose who you want to be part of the future of Blue Trail. The last director was there for how long?"

"Twenty-four years," Maria said.

"So, as long as you've been alive. Wow," Robyn said. "None of the campers or the counselors will have known anyone different. People will probably be a little apprehensive." Maria nodded. "But," Robyn continued, "if you're just yourself, everyone will go home and tell their families about how great you are. Still, priority number one is learning about the default state of this camp. Because if you don't know what needs to be fixed, or what the culture would be if you sat back and did nothing, you won't know what to do to bring it to where it needs to be." She paused before asking, "Do you remember JT?"

Maria did, though just barely. JT was the assistant director at Starry Sky during her first two summers as a camper, when she was 8 and 9 years old. She didn't have many memories with him one-on-one, but she remembered him making the announcements after every meal in the dining hall. He'd hold the floor like a true showman, making people laugh and cheer for even the most mundane housekeeping statements. However, in the last few years, whenever Robyn,

Lane, or even Maria herself, had grabbed the mic to make an announcement after a meal, it tended to take a bit of time for the unruly crowd of newly energized campers to settle down enough for their message to be heard, even with a mic. JT never had this difficulty. Everyone paid attention as soon as he raised the mic to his lips. Maria even remembered one of her cabinmates shushing her before he spoke once.

"JT wasn't a problem, was he? He retired in '08, right?" Maria asked.

"We asked him to retire after '08," Lane said with a grimace.

"Why?"

"It was four summers after I bought the camp from my parents," Lane explained. "We'd given him a lot of chances. He did a lot of things well. He was obviously great with helping the kids have fun and the counselors always felt supported by him. But he didn't take our feedback, nor did he give much feedback of his own to anyone. He'd let any project that took longer than five minutes slip through the cracks, and he was evasive when we'd check in, or even when we'd offer help. He'd been at the camp for ages and didn't seem to think that Robyn or I had much to offer as the new owners. This remained true even after we weren't so new anymore. It got to a point when we realized there were probably a lot of people out there who were good with kids—campers and counselors. But, like we've said, finding people who do that and fit in with the culture you're trying to build is the real challenge."

"It didn't seem like there was a lot of bad blood," Maria said. "He came back to visit, what, five summers in a row after he left?"

"Well, a year will do a lot to make someone remember the good times, I guess," Robyn said wryly. "It certainly seemed like there was going to be a lot of bad blood when we asked him to leave."

"Every camp team has a JT," Lane said. "And it might not be the first person you suspect. It's not always the least enthusiastic person, or the person who seems initially like they may not be pulling their weight, or the person who most adheres to the quote-unquote 'tradition.' People can change—if you're specific and consistent with what you ask them to change—those who can't or won't, those are your JTs."

"So I need to look out for my JTs," Maria said.

"The JTs, yes, but you need to know how everyone on your team profiles," Lane said. "And if there are people on your team who don't fit the profile of someone who's going to contribute positively ..."

"I don't want to clean house right away," Maria said.

"Maybe you won't have to," Robyn said charitably. "But say Blue Trail had a board and they had just fired their CEO. They'd be hiring you to step in and make the necessary changes. The old way wasn't working anymore."

"Yeah," Maria said, still thinking it all sounded a little cutthroat. Maybe it was foolish, but she really couldn't see any of the people she'd met at Blue Trail being as difficult as Robyn and Lane had described JT.

"Don't think of it as having to clean house," Lane said. "Think of it as being empowered, maybe even expected, to surround yourself with those who you know can do the job as you see it. Think of it as owing it to the campers, the counselors, the parents, and yourself—as the leader of the organization—to hire the people who will make the vision that you sell during recruiting visits a reality."

A bold thought nudged its way into Maria's head. She'd been playing with this idea for the last couple weeks, but until now, she wouldn't have dared ask. "Well, the person I trust the most, other than you all, is Samira."

Robyn and Lane looked at each other, grinning. "We were wondering whether you might inquire about her," Robyn said.

Samira was the social worker at Starry Sky. She had worked there for five summers now and she and Maria had hit it off since the first moment Samira set foot in the office. More importantly, she was an incredible worker and had nearly single-handedly solved some of Starry Sky's biggest emotional conflicts since arriving on staff. Counselors and campers alike loved and respected her. Maria thought of her as a mentor, despite the fact that Samira was just a few years her senior. She was the kind of person that helped everyone around her grow into the best version of themselves.

"I know she's happy at Starry Sky and I know you all love having her there, but I can't help but dream about having her on board at Blue Trail," Maria said.

A silence fell over the table. Robyn and Lane had already given Maria so much to help her achieve her dream. She felt bad even asking about poaching their best employee. But her mentors didn't look angry. Lane's lips were pursed, his eyes lost in thought.

"As camp directors, we'd hate to lose her," he admitted. "But given that we're now stakeholders in Blue Trail, it does seem like the fit couldn't have been better grown in a lab."

"I agree," Robyn said. "I can't say I'm rooting for her to leave Starry Sky, but you should call her. Make her a nice deal. If an independent person wants to take a competitive offer from another organization, we can't stop her, now, can we?"

It wasn't exactly shining encouragement, but Maria lit up just the same. "So, to be clear, you're okay with me making her an offer?" she clarified.

"Yes," Robyn said. "Maybe it's time for her to fly the coop as well. She'd be perfect for Blue Trail."

Maria was already imagining how she and Samira would bounce ideas off each other over lunch at the staff table in the dining hall, how much smoother it would be to form easy relationships with the counselors with her there. Samira was the type of worker every team needed. When she committed to do something, it was done and done well. When she saw something that needed solving, she took care of it. Robyn and Lane were offering someone who Maria viewed as their most valuable staff member. It was another stroke of unbelievable generosity. Excitement and gratitude brought a smile to Maria's face once again.

"I'll call her tomorrow," Maria said.

"Great choice," Robyn said.

"You know we're always going to be a resource for you," Lane said, looking at Maria intently. "And not just because our money is on the table, too. If there's anything we can do to help you out—a listening ear, a bit of advice, a connection to someone in the camping world, we'll do it. We owe you that much."

"You all don't owe me anything," Maria said. "You've given me quite enough."

"Suddenly, I feel like a toast is in order," Robyn said.

"Maybe that's our sign to head to dinner," Lane said.

"Sounds good to me," Maria said. She picked up the signed papers upon which her future was sealed and gently slid them back into the large envelope they'd been delivered in. Once the envelope was stowed safely inside her purse, the three directors stood from the big wooden table and departed to celebrate Maria's new camp properly.

Discussion activity 1.1

Reflect and Discuss:

Think: What are some positive and negative aspects of your current work culture?

Discuss: Are there unspoken "defaults" or "the way things have always been" that might be holding your team back? How can you challenge them constructively?

Challenge: Imagine you have a magic wand and could instantly change one thing about your team's culture. What would it be? Why? Now, take away the magic wand. Who would you need to get on board to make this change? What steps would you take to initiate this work?

Discussion activity 1.2

Unified Vision

Think: Briefly describe your organization's mission statement. Does it feel aspirational, clear, and relevant to everyone? Or does it sound like vague words on a dusty poster?

Discuss: Share your experiences with your organization's vision. Do you feel connected to it? In what ways does it—or could it—guide your everyday actions? Why or why not?
Leadership: How can leaders actively engage the team in defining, refining, and embodying the organization's vision?

Impact: Analyze the potential consequences of lacking a clear, unified vision. Consider issues like misalignment, decreased motivation, and missed opportunities. Flipping the question, what do you see as the main benefits to embracing a clear, unified vision?

CHAPTER 2
THE OFFER

THE next day, at the end of a morning jog in Robyn and Lane's neighborhood, Maria called Samira, prepared to give the pitch of a lifetime. She could feel her heartbeat all the way up in her head, and she was so excited to extend this offer to her friend that she didn't even go back inside to make the call; instead she scrolled through her contacts with cold, stiff fingers until she found Samira's name. She wouldn't have called anyone else this early, but Samira was a high school counselor, and Maria knew she liked to get up at the crack of dawn so she could arrive at her school early. Punctuality was one of her many strong suits.

Samira picked up on the second ring. "Maria! How's Tucson?"

"Cold, surprisingly. How are you doing?"

Samira laughed. "I'm doing well! School year's in full

swing, you know, but it's been pretty good. And it's not exam season yet, so hopefully there will be a few more weeks of calm before the storm."

"Glad to hear," Maria said. "So, um, I'll get right to it."

"Ooh!" Samira said, her voice rising a bit.

"Kelly's going to be taking over eventually at Starry Sky and even though it's hard for me to imagine working anywhere else, my dream has always been to own and direct my own camp. I didn't want to tell you until it was a done deal, but now it's safe to say that in about a week I will be the new owner of Camp Blue Trail in Wisconsin. Robyn and Lane have been supportive through this process. They even co-signed the loan with me."

"Maria, that's great! Oh, I'm so happy for you, I know you really wanted to run your own place. You deserve it."

"Thanks," Maria said. "It's a good camp. A lot of work to do, as you'd probably expect, but I liked the leadership team when I met them a while back and the place is beautiful. I'm excited to get started. But, honestly, I'm pretty nervous to walk into the summer without really knowing who I can trust."

"I get that. I'm sure it feels daunting," Samira replied. "But everyone knows you've got what it takes to succeed."

"Thank you," Maria said again. "But I can only imagine the challenges that will soon be mine to solve. I would feel more confident about this transition if I knew that I had somebody like you on board. Which brings me to why I called you—I wanted to ask if you'd be willing to come with me to Blue Trail."

"Oh my gosh, Maria ..."

"I know that it's a huge ask," Maria said. "But Robyn and Lane gave me a lot of good advice yesterday, and first and foremost was to surround myself with people who I trust and share my vision and aspirations for Blue Trail. And I know you do, because so much of what I believe makes a great camp came straight from you."

"This isn't some fancy way of them firing me, is it?"

"Oh no, I think they'd sooner sell the camp than fire you.

I wouldn't have dreamed of asking you to leave Starry Sky unless they approved and I honestly didn't think there was any way, but here we are. This genuinely seems to be out of the goodness of their hearts. One of many things they're doing for me out of the goodness of their hearts, I guess. So ... thoughts?"

"I'm interested, of course. Working with you at a new camp," Samira trailed off. "It would be amazing. I can't believe this."

Maria smiled into the phone. She didn't know anyone quite like Samira, with such an ebullient exterior buoyed by depths of knowledge. Blue Trail didn't know how lucky it was to have a chance at gaining her services.

"I can take a look at the books again today and send you a more official proposal," Maria said. "Times are obviously a little tough, or else they probably wouldn't be selling, but I can promise to at least match your current pay."

"Okay, yeah," Samira said. "Thank you. That's a good start and I'd love to hear more. And I think I should give Robyn and Lane a call. But I'd really love to build something with you, if that's what you want."

"Are you kidding?" Maria said. "You'd be numbers one through five on my list of top five choices for a social worker."

"Well, thank you. That means a lot."

"Of course. Do you want to talk again tomorrow or the day after, about the details of what I send over? I can answer any questions you have about Blue Trail, or the job, or anything else you're curious about then."

"Tomorrow works. If you're up early again tomorrow, you can call me then, though depending on when you send the offer over today, it might work better if you call me after school gets out, so I have time to look it all over."

"I'll call in the afternoon, then. Looking forward to it. Thank you so much, Samira."

"No, thank you! Looking forward to talking more! Bye, Maria!"

Maria hung up, feeling relieved. She hadn't quite realized how nervous she'd been feeling before she made that call. If Samira had been tepid, it would've been a blow. Even though she'd bought the camp assuming she wouldn't be taking any of Starry Sky's wonderful team with her, it would've been different if she'd offered a position to one of her former coworkers and been rebuffed. Samira's enthusiasm made Maria feel like she had one more person in her corner, one more person who had confidence in the camp she was going to remake.

When Maria got inside, she put a pot of water on the stove and retrieved her laptop to look over Blue Trail's budget. Predictably, there wasn't a lot of room to offer Samira a cushy salary. But, she knew that she needed to offer something respectful and rewarding. Switching camps would be a risk for Samira, as well. While Maria's appreciation would be shown in many ways, and she believed that on a personal level, Samira would like to work with her, she knew the financial piece would be an important factor in her friend's decision.

Maria was relieved to see there would be enough room in the budget to pay Samira what she earned at Starry Sky, if Maria was willing to take a smaller draw for herself. The previous director at Blue Trail had been taking out almost twice what Robyn and Lane earned at Starry Sky. Perhaps it made sense—Blue Trail was a well-known camp and the fact he was selling probably meant that he was investing less in infrastructure. Maria could certainly make do with less, especially if it meant that she had room to sweeten a deal for Samira.

Maria could also offer a 3 percent raise per summer, provided they could stem Blue Trail's retention and enrollment losses, or at least keep them from worsening after her first year. She didn't know precisely how much Samira's salary was climbing per year at Starry Sky, but 3 percent was what her own salary was raised by each year and she felt comfortable giving that to Samira as well.

Barring any further enrollment catastrophe, there would even be enough money to offer Samira a $10,000 bonus for being part of the transition, awarded after Samira's third summer. Maria felt satisfied with this offer. Changing jobs was never easy, but camping was a little different. Samira wouldn't have to move, nor leave her primary job at the high school. And she would have the ability to make an immediate impact on hundreds of new campers and counselors each year.

Between the matching salary, the raises, and the bonus, it was a compelling offer. She might have been biased, or overly hopeful, but Maria thought she'd accept the offer herself, if she were in Samira's shoes. She opened up a document and typed out all the details in a much more official manner than the sticky note she'd been writing on. Once she was finished, she attached it to an email and sent it off to Samira, hoping that the fact that she'd sent it before it was even midday would underscore how serious she was about wanting Samira to join her at Blue Trail.

Samira didn't respond until the evening. When Maria got the notification on her phone, she eagerly opened the email and read:

Hi Maria!

This offer looks great! I'm pleased that you'll be able to match what I'm currently paid at Starry Sky and that there is ample opportunity for an increase in pay. As I know you are, too, I am saddened by the thought of leaving Starry Sky, but excited by the possibility of working with you to create something special. I would love to talk tomorrow about what you envision for my responsibilities and how we would work together to achieve our shared vision. Unless you tell me something insane tomorrow, I'm in.

Thank you,
Samira

Maria smiled at the last line of the message. Needless to say, she didn't intend on dropping any huge new elements of the job description on her tomorrow. But she did intend to be very clear about what she expected from Samira in their first summer together at Blue Trail. That said, if Samira came into Blue Trail and did the exact same work she did at Starry Sky, they'd be in great shape.

The next afternoon, Maria picked up the phone and called Samira once again. It was Maria's last day in Tucson before she headed back up to her own non-camp life in Phoenix, and she was pleased to be taking care of this last, most important piece of business yet. It had been a very productive few days, soaking up all the wisdom she could from Robyn and Lane while they attended to everything they needed to do in order for Maria to officially take the helm at Blue Trail.

"So, are you feeling good about the official offer?" Maria asked Samira.

"Yeah, the offer is great," Samira said. "I'm just curious to hear more about what you think needs to happen to get Blue Trail back on its feet. What are you going to do, summer one, to start turning things around?"

Maria contemplated. It was a weighty question, clearly. She didn't want to jump straight in and trail off, or seem unprepared. She sometimes had a habit of talking before she'd formed a full thought. Some would say it's enthusiasm. Maria disliked it about herself. It had gotten better as she'd gotten a bit older, but it still felt like a very young thing about her.

"Well, here's the thing," Maria said. "I haven't spent much time with the leadership team yet. Obviously I haven't worked with them at all, I just got the ownership papers the other day. So, other than a few dollar figures and enrollment numbers, I don't have a super specific picture of what needs to change."

"Sure," Samira said. It didn't sound sarcastic and Maria didn't interpret it as such. It sounded like she could truly understand the scenario.

"Which leads me to my first goal, goal one of three for our first summer: observe. This is basically straight from Robyn and Lane, as well. They strongly encouraged me to do as much observing as possible. I need to understand the default way of life at Blue Trail. I need to know what got them to this point. I want to understand how all the dynamics on our staff work without being too much of a disruptor."

"Okay," Samira said. "I can see the rest of the team appreciating non-disruption."

"I hope so," Maria said. "But I can also see that a desire to sit back and observe could be a strange look. I don't want to observe at the expense of actually directing. There are going to be things we see that could be done differently and I can't shy away from addressing those. So it'll be a delicate line to walk, which leads me to goal number two: building relationships. The last director was there for twenty years. I have no idea what he did to get off on the right foot at the start of his tenure, but I know that by the end he was pretty beloved, even though behind the scenes, things were a struggle. He's leaving some big shoes and I've got to fill them in a different way with the campers than I do with the staff and parents."

"How big is the camp?"

"Last summer? A little less than three hundred campers, and sixty-five staff. Ideally, we'd get up to four hundred campers and eighty staff."

"Ah. Work to do."

"Yes indeed and lots of people to get to know. And I intend to get to know all of them, as much as a director of that many people can. So, building relationships—I'm going to learn every camper's name by week one and engage each one in a meaningful one-on-one conversation during the summer. Same thing with the staff, we've got to have an open dialogue with everyone on the team. They have to feel like they can trust me, because I want and need to hear their thoughts on how camp is working great and how it could be working better. And we need to be able to work together to solve problems as they come up."

"Of course."

"We're camp experts, but they're the Blue Trail experts.

They're going to be the ones teaching us summer one. And, as appreciation for that, this summer and every summer, I'm going to create a positive environment for staff through feedback, bonding events, theme days, anything we can think of to create an environment of trust. I'll need your help with that."

See discussion activity 2.1 at the end of the chapter

"Sounds like it's right up my alley," Samira said. "We should bring Staff Field Day to Blue Trail, for the end of staff training."

"I was thinking about that as well," Maria said. "Funny enough, we've arrived now at goal number three: ensure the safety and well-being of everyone at camp."

Samira hmmed in agreement at this point, the most important part of her job.

"At the most basic level," Maria continued, "Summer one will be a success if, beyond the inevitable scrapes and squabbles that come with any camp, there aren't any major physical, emotional, or professional emergencies. To that end, I need to learn about how staff training has been done at Blue Trail in the past, but I can tell you that I want to bring every safety protocol we had at Starry Sky over to Blue Trail."

"Cheers to that," Samira said. "Do you see me taking on the same responsibilities as I had at Starry Sky in terms of emotional support and conflict resolution and the like?"

"Absolutely. I can't think of anyone better. Camp should be a space where people can grow, and we need someone who's great at the emotional support side of things to accomplish that goal."

"Awesome. I agree."

Maria had never thought of herself as someone who was amazing at the tough emotional stuff. It wasn't that she was dispassionate or prickly, she had a decent understanding of the theory behind all of what Samira did, but that was a very different thing than responding skillfully when a camper came to you with tears in their eyes and a serious issue to get off their chest. Samira was much better at threading that needle between helping someone find a solution productively and listening enough so they felt validated. Not only that, she was good at sharing the techniques she knew so well with counselors, too.

"That was the thing I liked best about Starry Sky; when I was a camper, when I was a counselor, and when I was assistant director, all the way through," Maria said. "It helped people grow."

Fond memories were resurfacing as she spoke. Yes, Robyn remembered Maria's eight-year-old self correctly. In large groups, she was gregarious and confident. But in the smaller moments, she was quite shy and anxious. There had been a lot of fears that camp had helped her overcome. She was scared of swimming if it wasn't in a pool, scared of the dark, scared of new foods. Whether it was through the gentle nudge of a counselor or the shouted encouragement of her friends, she'd gotten past a lot of things that would've continued to hold her back if it hadn't been for camp.

Starry Sky had a detoxifying effect; she saw it with herself and the campers. Every summer, it felt like Maria was bringing some new spiritual bug from the year into camp, and every summer, she left camp feeling lighter. She became braver as a youth, more secure as a teenager, and more competent as an adult.

Camp, she felt, was unique in this regard. School could be bruising, other jobs too unsatisfying. There was a reason why so many people found it so hard to leave the camping world. There weren't that many other jobs, in Maria's view, that left one feeling so fulfilled, so much stronger, once they finished their work.

Samira echoed her thoughts. "I think I'm a much better person than I would've been without Starry Sky."

"You were already a plenty-good person the moment you arrived at Starry Sky," Maria said. "But, camp really is profound this way."

"Well, I can't say I'm surprised, but you really have thought things out," Samira said. On the other end, Maria relaxed in her chair, not realizing how upright she'd been sitting. "It would be an honor to be a part of Blue Trail's very bright future."

"Really?" Maria exclaimed.

"Yes, for real. Let's do this. When can I start?"

Discussion activity 2.1

Untapped Potential:
Leveraging Hidden Expertise Across All Levels

Think: Can expertise truly reside only at the top of the organizational pyramid? Consider examples where valuable knowledge and insights came from unexpected sources within your own experience.

Discuss: Share past situations where you witnessed talent and potential underutilized due to rigid hierarchies or assumptions about expertise based on position.

Challenge: How can you actively seek out and leverage expertise from individuals at all levels, not just those in senior positions?

The Cost of Neglect: Consider the potential negative consequences of ignoring this diverse expertise, such as missed opportunities, innovation stagnation and employee disengagement.

Leadership Strategies: How can leaders create an environment where everyone feels empowered to share their expertise, regardless of their position?

CHAPTER 3

WHAT WE LOVE ABOUT CAMP

MARIA adjusted her desk lamp and checked her image in the little box in the corner of her screen. She made sure she could easily read her notes and the agenda, with the document open on half of the screen and the video call on the other. Ordinarily, she took notes by hand, but she thought it would look the tiniest bit more professional to look off to the side slightly for reference, rather than looking down at her desk or her lap. The document was packed. They had a lot to cover and she wanted to present a prepared energy to her team right from the get-go. This wasn't just a meet-and-greet. Beyond the agenda she'd sent out, Maria looked at this meeting as a chance to set the beginnings of an agenda for next summer, as well. She'd opened the meeting a few minutes before their agreed-upon time, curious to see whether anyone else would log on early. So far, nobody was an early bird.

It had been interesting and mildly amusing finding a time that could work for everyone. All five other leadership team members had either day jobs or school and nobody was in the same city as she was. Maria wasn't like some corporate boss who could simply call a meeting at a certain time and expect everyone to be there, especially in the off season. But on this Tuesday evening in February, they'd found a time that worked for their first meeting as one leadership team. Maria managed her nerves, reminding herself that surely everyone else would be just as eager to bring their best selves to the meeting.

Suddenly, a flurry of notifications materialized at the top of the screen as everyone seemed to join at once. Maria clicked the "admit" button as fast as it appeared for each name. Jamie's face popped into the meeting, then Samira's, then Stu's, Laverne's, and Nico's. They were off to an auspicious start; everyone was on time to their first staff meeting.

"How's everyone doing?" Maria asked. She was met with a chorus of "Good" and "Great" and one "Dandy, how about yourself?" from Stu. Maria noticed that a few people muted themselves after answering her greeting.

"I think we can all stay off mute," Maria said. "There aren't a lot of us and I want everyone to feel like they can just jump in." One by one, the little red mic symbols by everyone's names disappeared.

See discussion activity 3.1 at the end of the chapter

"Great," Maria said. "So, I know most of you are quite familiar with each other, and I met a few of you already, but just so we can all get officially acquainted ..." Maria noticed Samira smile slightly. "As per the agenda, I think we should introduce ourselves. I'm sure everyone recognizes a new face, Samira, whose introduction I will add a bit to after she introduces herself. If you all can forgive a little corniness, can we each say one thing we love about Blue

Trail or camping in general? I'd love to know what every-one loves about what we do."

Maria had braced for an awkward silence after she fin-ished speaking, but luckily Nico leaned forward in his chair and smiled brightly.

"Um, hi," he started. "I'm Nico, I'm trips director, so … I'm a big fan of our trips." Maria and a few others chuckled.

"I have a lot of friends who work at other camps and I just feel like we're really lucky to have the program that we do here," Nico continued. "They tell me what the trips are like where they work and I just think to myself, 'Man, I'm really glad I'm at Blue Trail.' We go to more places, we spend more time in these places, and almost every trip we send out is completely full. We've done well selling trips as a big part of the Blue Trail experience.

"I remember when I was a camper and I'd be on trips with people, and by the end of the trip they'd all be com-pletely different people than when we started; you know, stronger, happier, more confident. Maybe it's a little cliché, but I think the best thing we offer people is the ability to get out into nature and find some new gear within themselves that they didn't know they had. Whatever growth they were already going to have at camp, it's like, accelerated when they're out on a trip."

"Yeah, Nico, can I just jump in?" Jamie began. "You're being really nice to say that 'we' have done well selling trips as part of Blue Trail, but I think we can all agree that last summer was an all-time great summer for trips. Sometimes I'd look around the picnic area and I'd be like, 'Oh my gosh, where did everyone go?' And it just so happened to be your first summer as trips director, the first summer we had anyone as a trips director, so give yourself a bit of credit, man. You were out there putting in the work. Kudos."

Nico put his hands together in a prayer gesture and smiled across cyberspace at Jamie. Maria felt a strange urge to applaud. She, of course, hadn't borne witness to this sup-posed sea change in trips culture, but she was thrilled at the spontaneous and sincere positivity.

"Okay, thanks, Nico," Maria said. "And, yeah, I agree. In my experience, the kids who do trips get a lot of positive outcomes out of their camp experience, so to have such a good program here is really amazing. I don't think I really knew how good it was at Blue Trail, and I'm hyped to learn more about where we go and what trips look like here." Nico nodded, seemingly satisfied with her praise. "Does anyone feel like going next?"

"Sure," Stu said. "I'm Stu, parent liaison. I could obviously say my favorite part of Blue Trail is getting to spend my summers in the sun and the trees and on the lake, and getting to see kids having the time of their lives with their friends, but I think I'll go with the fact that my job allows me to share with parents our excitement on the growth that their kids achieve every day they're with us."

"Hear, hear," Samira said.

"Thanks for sharing," Maria said. When she asked for a volunteer, nobody spoke right away. After a few seconds, Samira read her mind and jumped in.

"Hi! I'm Samira," she said. "I'm Blue Trail's new social worker. I'm a high school counselor in the offseason and before this I worked at Camp Starry Sky with Maria. I love the bonds I get to build with the kids and, even though part of my job is to help them in the low moments, I love when they run up and tell me some cool thing they did or experience they had, because they want to share their high moments too. I'm really looking forward to working with all of you. Maria has told me great things about you. Oh, and our counselors — which is another favorite part of my job — working with them, but I'll let someone else talk. And if anyone has questions about what a social worker does at camp, I'd be happy to answer them. I'll drop my email and number in the chat."

"I appreciate hearing that, Samira," Maria said. "Glad to have you working with us. And I can say, from my personal experience with Samira, that she's one of the most emotionally intelligent, hardest-working, easy going people I've ever worked with. So I'm really happy that she decided to join us here at Blue Trail."

"Welcome, Samira!" Jamie said. Stu and Nico hooted in assent. Samira smiled.

There were only two people left aside from Maria, so she sat back and waited for one of them to speak up, which Laverne did in short order.

"Hey everyone, I'm Laverne, I'm the activities director. I came to Blue Trail just after my three kiddos left Blue Trail, so between all of us, this camp's been in our family for over thirty years." Her voice was gruff and no-nonsense, but Maria was rather impressed; it was a heartwarming way of putting it. Laverne continued. "The two other old-timers here know this already and Nico knows it because he was one of 'em, but a lot of campers call me 'Mama V' because somehow I ended up being the one-stop shop for homesick kids."

"Hey, that was a long time ago," Nico protested.

"Not long enough for me to forget it," Laverne said. The others were laughing, even Samira. "But, hey, if they think I'm the one who's gonna make them feel better, I'm more than happy to oblige. I remember reading the letters from my own kids telling me how much they missed me when they were at camp, and during the school year, they wouldn't have been caught dead telling me anything as sweet, so I like to do my best to remind the kids at camp that Mom and Pop will be waiting for them at home and they'd want them to be having fun and making lots of new friends."

"That's really sweet," Maria said. "I'm glad to hear that." Laverne put up a heart emoji in her box on the screen.

"Jamie?" Maria prompted.

Jamie took a long, deep breath before beginning. "I might end up repeating what everyone else has said, but I really do feel this way. I remember everyone who's come to this camp since I've been here. Like you said, Samira, I've seen a lot of high moments and a lot of low moments and I enjoy being there for all of them. It just really feeds my soul."

Maria thought it somehow sounded a little less genuine coming from Jamie than Samira. Maybe it was just the repetition, but the way he was talking made Maria think that, as a camper, she'd rather have Samira in her corner than Jamie.

Samira seemed just a little more altruistic. But she checked her face in her onscreen box. She betrayed no judgment.

"But for me," Jamie said. "I love the campfires. I just do. And who doesn't? All the songs, the stories, the smell of the fire and the sound of laughter. We all get to come together every Saturday night and just enjoy the energy of our brothers and sisters. It's special."

"I can't wait for my first Blue Trail campfire," Maria said diplomatically. She noticed that Laverne and Nico were both stone-faced. Maybe they weren't particularly impressed either.

"Okay, well, that just leaves me," she said. "I'm Maria, I've been the assistant director at Starry Sky for the past five summers and I've been in the camping world since I was eight years old. I'm overjoyed to get the opportunity to be a part of Blue Trail; I've heard so many amazing things about this camp—even before the possibility of buying the camp came about. I'm sure I'll have many favorite things about Blue Trail by the time this summer is over, but for now, I'll say that my favorite thing about camping in general is that it's just an immensely valuable experience for people at any age. Every time I've come back to camp, whether as a little kid, a teenager, or an adult in a leadership position, camp somehow knows exactly what I need to grow and feel good and I end the summer feeling, well, like Nico said, stronger, happier, and more confident.

"And I want you all to know, I wasn't just asking about that for good vibes," Maria continued. "I think it's important to talk about what we love about camp. I suspected there would be a lot of commonalities and there absolutely were. Most of us—except Jamie, a little voice in Maria's head said—talked about growth in one form or another. Nico said that he's seen kids really find themselves on trips. Laverne talked about helping kids be more independent. I'm glad that we're all noticing this growth, noticing how valuable it is. I want to keep keying in on that as we get closer to summer and especially while we're in the summer."

There was a fluttering of nods and Maria sat up straighter in her chair, pleased that this experienced team seemed to be digesting what she had to say.

Norms and Expectations

Maria starts the meeting by setting one basic expectation. She'll need to circle back to create a more robust list of norms and expectations for meetings.

Think: What are the potential consequences of not clearly setting norms and expectations in a work team? Consider decreased productivity, communication issues, and conflict.

Challenge: How can you move beyond vague statements like "respect each other" and define clear, actionable norms for your team?

Brainstorm: Develop a list of between three to five essential norms that would significantly improve the effectiveness and well-being of your team.

Analyze: How does your leadership style influence the establishment and enforcement of team norms? What could you do differently? Are there ways that you could do a better job upholding the agreed-upon norms through your own actions and communication?

CHAPTER 4
CHALLENGES

MOVING on to item two, then," Maria said. "I'd like to talk about our biggest challenges at camp. The reason being, just, like with our favorite things, I expect some overlap with our challenges, as well. And if there are challenges for us, they could be obstacles to retaining and recruiting campers and staff."

"Very true," Jamie said.

"I'll go first," Maria said. "I personally don't feel as strong with helping campers or counselors who are in an emotional crisis. If a counselor comes to me with a procedural question or a kid comes up just wanting to talk or joke around, I'm fine. But when it comes to thornier stuff, let's just say I'm no Samira. I understand all the theory, you know; I've been to trainings in and outside of camp on the social-emotional side of things, but it still feels really tough to find the right words when I'm in the heat of the moment. I'm afraid of saying something wrong and therefore don't end up saying anything that's truly right."

Maria took a breath. It felt good to show a bit of vulnerability in front of her new team, but she had to remember to show herself some empathy, too. There were others on this team and at Starry Sky, who were better at this than her and that was okay. There were counselors who lived with the kids every day. This perceived weakness hadn't prevented her from rising to this level, but that didn't mean she could give herself a pass on this issue in perpetuity.

"I know it's important for me to learn this skill, because part of a director's job is to help everyone else at camp feel like they're seen and supported, and kids don't want to go to camp at a place where they don't know that the director has their back 100 percent."

Maria felt a little drained, but also relieved. She hoped that even though this was their first meeting as one Blue Trail team, the others on the call would also reflect as deeply as she did.

See discussion activity 4.1 at the end of the chapter

"All right, I yield the floor," Maria said.

"I'll take a stab at it," Stu said, a bemused grin playing across his face. "I'm not saying my job is unique in this regard, but it is a hard job. Ideally, we have about four hundred campers and eighty staff. That's quite a few parents to deal with. I get emails and calls every day, naturally, and I feel confident in my ability to communicate when I have all the information, but there are many times where I don't feel like I have all the necessary information to reassure a parent that everything is going smoothly, and that's a less-than-ideal look for me and, more importantly, for the camp.

"Now, I take ownership of this," Stu said, and Maria appreciated that he took the time to ensure that nobody else felt thrown under the bus, even implicitly. "I could've been more proactive in the past to establish a system that gets me basic information about campers and counselors' well-being, day in and day out. But, given our fresh start here, I'll just put that out there as something that would make my job a whole lot less challenging."

See discussion activity 4.2 at the end of the chapter

"Okay," Maria said. "That's a great thing to reflect on, Stu, thank you. I've definitely heard of some good systems that address this exact problem. As you might suspect, this isn't a challenge unique to Blue Trail."

"I figured as much," Stu said. "One thing I'd like to do before camp starts is create a system that counselors could use to give me quick updates on challenges they are facing with campers, so I can be proactive in communicating with parents. I'll brainstorm something before we meet next and I'd love it if everyone could chip in with some feedback on whether it seems feasible for their departments to implement."

"You anticipated my next question," Maria said, grinning. "I was gonna ask what we can accomplish toward this before camp starts." She typed out a note below the end of the agenda reminding herself to loop back with Stu to see if he needed any help with the brainstorming. "I think it'd be great to workshop some ideas at the next meeting."

"I can go next, if we're ready to move on," Nico said.

"Please," Maria said.

"I think the biggest challenge with trips is gonna be building off of last summer, considering how many people were interested and jazzed about getting out into nature with us. Like, how do we take that to the next level?"

Unlike Nico's previous answer, the call was silent for this one. It was exactly the kind of answer Maria was hoping people would avoid. Vague and a touch self-aggrandizing. It wasn't that she wanted people to deprecate their own work from the prior summer, but there was always room for improvement. And, although it could be tough or awkward in the moment of prompted reflection, the more specific that people were with their introspection, the easier it would be to address the challenges they identified.

Maria decided to start her response on a positive note. "I'm really glad to hear that last summer felt like a sea change for trips. I want to celebrate that success," she said. "Maybe we can shift to the sort of hidden part two of my question, which would be what ideas do you have to address this challenge? When you say 'building off of last summer,' does anything spring to mind right off the bat?"

Nico looked down at his lap. "Umm," he started. Maria felt a twinge of regret. Had she boxed him in? Then, he looked back up at the camera. "I'm thinking about some of our lower-level trips, the ones aimed at younger campers. They're aimed at the littles for a reason, but they're still really cool trips. I don't have the precise numbers, but even though trip participation on the whole was way up last summer, the shorter trips were significantly less popular than the longer, more older-kid-oriented ones. So, if we want kids of all ages taking lots of trips, which we do, because we value what kids learn on trips, I think during staff training I should get the counselors in the younger cabins on board with pushing trips as a big Blue Trail experience."

Maria made another note on her document. "That sounds logical to me. I know this isn't a problem unique to Blue Trail, younger kids often are just a little more nervous to leave camp, since camp itself is already a huge change for them. But there are definitely ways to get them pumped up about the idea. Thanks, Nico. Let me know if I can help with devising any of the messaging you want to put out."

"Will do," Nico said.

"I got something," Laverne said. "It always feels like there's one or two activities a year that don't have great people leading them. Waterskiing, obviously, somebody capable is there. Basketball, baseball, soccer, not usually a problem. They're popular enough. A lot of the other ones, though, it feels like a crapshoot whether we're gonna get someone on staff who can teach it."

Maria saw Jamie's jaw clench.

"We've talked about this before," he said. "My thinking is that the most important thing is to hire skilled and empa-

thetic counselors. If there's room for a few activity specialists, great, but we sort of get what we get. And I don't say
that to be lazy, but it's true."

"I wasn't calling you out, Jamie," Laverne said. "I'm just
saying, that's a challenge for me. I'm drawing up who's
gonna go where and it gets to a point where it's like my third
best choice for their seventh-ranked preference or something. How did we get to that point?"

Maria's eyes instinctively met Samira's. They seemed to
be on the same page that, unless Maria said something, there
was about to be an actual argument.

"So what I'm hearing," Maria said, "is that Laverne feels
like it's a challenge to match staff members to activities
they're truly qualified to teach or run, and Jamie feels like a
decision was made in the past that the priority with hiring
was to find skilled counselors first, and activity leaders second. Does that ring true?"

"That's what we decided on," Jamie said.

"Yes ma'am," Laverne said. Neither of them sounded entirely pleased to have to clarify.

"Laverne, is this something you feel we need to revisit?"
Maria asked.

"I think it would be smart," she replied. "Or maybe I'm
just biased toward my field." She gave a theatrical shrug.

"Well, yeah, it is your field, but we're talking about challenges, so if this is something that's been a struggle, I think
we need to unpack it."

"Maria, if I may," Jamie said. "I think this is a bigger discussion than just one part of one meeting."

"We're all here, aren't we?" Laverne replied coolly.

Jamie sat up straighter in his chair, leaning closer to his
camera.

"All right. Here's my take," he said. "Laverne's right that
it's important to have people who know what they're doing
for a few activities. Waterskiing, for example; people have to
know how to drive a boat and teach kids how to get up and
not get a concussion. Most of the sports, yeah, they're like
this, too. Our kids deserve to get better at the things they

sign up for. But, if we have four people assigned each period to tennis, is it important that each of them earned a scholarship to a Division 1 school? I think not."

"Oh, come on," Laverne said. "You know that's not what I'm saying. I just think that when people check all those little boxes for skills on the application, they should be able to back them up. Or, if they don't check any of those little boxes, maybe they aren't a great fit for Camp Blue Trail."

"I disagree," Jamie said, throwing his hands up. "I just disagree. That's not the way we've thought about things in the past. Blue Trail staff members are exceptional—professionally, relationally, personally—I just can't wrap my head around the idea that that's somehow untrue just because they aren't experts in our least popular activities."

"Couldn't we find some exceptional people who can also lead an activity well?" Laverne asked.

"I think it would be news to a lot of our counselors that they were leading their activities so badly."

"Why would it be news? Because you didn't give them any feedback?" Laverne retorted.

"I'm not the activities director," Jamie said. "I give them feedback all the time on other stuff!"

As Jamie spoke, Samira's gaze was practically begging Maria to redirect the conversation and although Maria was never inclined to stop a healthy discussion, she was now beginning to agree with Jamie's initial assertion that this was too big of a topic for this one meeting. The disagreement was starting to spiral into broader aspersions about each of their job performances. Maria had subconsciously clenched her jaw. She hoped that this was not how this team usually navigated disagreement.

"I think it would be a good idea to come back to this at another time," Maria said, before Laverne could get her next barb in. "It's a very important discussion and it probably requires more space than we have on the agenda right now to address it.

"As you all know, I'm coming in unaware of any past discussions on this issue, but it seems like we could explore the possibility of hiring some pure activity specialists without increasing payroll, though that would mean sacrificing counselors, which I'm less inclined to do. So we'll circle back. But thank you for sharing this challenge, Laverne."

"You got it," Laverne said curtly.

"And I mean it, we will circle back," Maria said. She didn't want to seem like she was afraid of disagreement. She definitely wasn't. At Starry Sky, she'd borne witness to and even been a part of several heated discussions, including with Robyn and Lane. Disagreement wasn't an issue, at least when it was actually about an issue.

"Jamie and Laverne, I really do appreciate you both bringing this up. I think the direction we choose will affect a lot of things—how we market camp, what the culture is like, what kind of people we attract—and I don't think there is a wrong answer, but it seems like, even if this was discussed in the past . . ."

"It wasn't," Laverne interrupted.

"Yeah, it was, five years ago!" Jamie said.

"Five years ago? That would be an eternity even if we weren't bleeding campers," Laverne retorted.

"Even if this was discussed in the past," Maria repeated, speaking louder. "I think we can all agree that it seems wise to discuss it again, in a more dedicated time window. So I'm going to add it to the agenda for our next meeting and beforehand, I'm going to circulate some specific questions for everyone to consider before we talk about it."

"Everyone?" Nico asked.

"Everyone," Maria said. "I don't think any conflict of ideas on this team should be a one on one. We all have different responsibilities, but we're all working toward the same goal, so we all have valuable input on this issue. But, again, I'm grateful to you, Jamie and Laverne, for being willing to engage and voice your opinions on what the right direction is.

See discussion activity 4.3 at the end of the chapter

Neither of them said anything. Jamie graced her with a nod. On one hand, Maria was grateful that there didn't seem to be much ideological apathy on this team; on the other, it might be useful for her, or Samira, to lead off the next meeting—which was shaping up to be a bit of a showdown—with a crash course on how to work through the tension that naturally occurs in teams that collaborate well.

"Samira, maybe you want to share next?" Maria asked beseechingly.

"Sure," Samira said. "I've got a couple things, one of which might sound a little complain-y, so I'm trying to balance it out." Everyone laughed, though Maria tensed up, wondering what Samira might be wanting to get off her chest. "And I guess they kind of play into each other, but anyway, sometimes the job of a social worker, especially in this camp setting, can feel a little isolating. Don't get me wrong, I love it, and I feel confident with it, and I am grateful for all the work I've done in this position. The challenge for me is overcoming the feeling that I'm only ever really needed when there's a problem, or when there's training to be done. I know I talked earlier about seeing when people grow, especially campers, and I do see that, but it's also kind of circumstantial. Like, sometimes a kid will run up and tell me about some cool thing they did that we had worked on or that I helped them prepare for. But sometimes they won't. Sometimes they want nothing to do with me.

"And it's a similar issue with counselors," Samira continued. "I do my workshops or professional development and send them off into their cabins with what I hope are useful tools, but I don't really see them putting the tools into action, even though I know they are. So, I know it's the job, but yeah, sometimes I wish I was out and about a little more, so I could see that what I'm doing is working." As Samira was finishing, Stu and Jamie were snapping their fingers in support of what she was saying and Samira looked relieved.

Maria was surprised to hear all this from Samira. It sounded like she was asking for a little more responsibility; at Starry Sky, Samira had never given any indication that she felt this way. But Maria wrote in italics on her document, "May need to talk one-on-one w/Sam about her job." If Samira had ideas for ways she could be more front-facing, Maria was all ears. Samira had earned the right to make a pitch.

"I hear that, Samira," Maria said. "It's very understandable to want to see your work in action. And I think part of that would be bridging the knowledge you're offering over into the actual culture of Blue Trail. Why should the fruits of your labor be restricted to individual people implementing individual strategies? Same thing for everyone on this call. Everyone deserves to see the impact of their work campwide. That's important."

"Oh, it's not that I feel like I'm not making an impact," Samira said. "I don't know, this was hard to phrase." It was an odd thing to say, considering part of Samira's job was teaching people how to phrase things politely.

"Okay," Maria said. "Well, we can definitely talk more privately." Samira nodded. "Jamie, finish us off, if you would," Maria hoped he wouldn't dig up the fight with Laverne again.

"Sure," Jamie said. "I mean, it's been getting harder to hire counselors, and though I don't really have any data for this, it feels like, anecdotally, our cabin teams aren't as close-knit as they once were."

"Do you have any specific stories that made you feel this way?" Maria asked.

"Well," Jamie said, considering. "I'm not hearing as many fun night off stories."

"They're not going to tell their boss they went to a bar," Laverne said. Nico guffawed, but Jamie scowled.

"I have to believe they were omitting bar stories before as well," Jamie said tersely. "I don't know, in the past it hasn't been hard to see the bonds forming. Returning counselors would take new ones under their wings, and within, like, a week, it would seem like everyone was a pro, everyone was truly part of the fabric of Camp Blue Trail. I'm just not seeing that as much anymore. I wish I could be more specific, but maybe you'll see what I mean once the summer starts. Or maybe it'll be better this year, but I imagine you saw ebbs and flows with this sort of camaraderie at Starry Sky, too?"

"Yeah, there were definitely some summers where the staff felt tighter than others," Maria said. She wanted to dig a little deeper, though. "If you had to wager a guess, what would you say the issue might be?"

Jamie sighed. "I think it goes back to the issue that we all know the whole camp is facing. Retention. We're getting fewer counselors coming back for multi-year stints, which makes the staff less close, makes my off-season work more stressful, and honestly, decreases the overall quality of the staff. Even though a lot of the new people we hire turn out to be fantastic, we're missing that continuity, that veteran leadership, which would really improve the overall vibe year over year."

"That's an important insight," Maria said. "And, to be clear, this should not be public knowledge, or disseminated among the rest of the staff, but we will naturally be coming back to the retention issue a lot. It's existential, or, at least, if it doesn't get solved, Blue Trail will change pretty drastically. But I want to go back to something you said a minute ago, about data."

"I can speak a little to this," Stu said. "We send out two surveys at the end of every summer, one to counselors and one to parents. Campers complete small surveys on their last day of the session. The counselor survey is mostly about whether they felt supported as employees, and the parent survey for counselors is basically a slimmed down version of the one they fill out for campers. A lot of the counselors are young enough where parents are still looking at camp as a developmental experience for them, rather than a real summer job."

"Where is all the data from these surveys stored?" Maria asked.

"It's in our shared drive," Stu said. "I'll send you a link."

"Yeah, I'd love to see it," Maria said. "Beyond each of our ideas and expertise, that data needs to inform a lot of what we do to boost our enrollment numbers. And, Jamie, I think what you're talking about is definitely quantifiable. If there isn't a question on this counselor survey about how close they feel to other members of the staff, there should be. Is there?"

Jamie and Stu both shook their heads.

Maria continued, "Maybe it could be like, 'Rate 1 to 10 how close you feel to the rest of the staff.' Or, 'I strongly disagree to strongly agree with the statement, I have at least three coworkers I would call friends.' Or, 'I felt like my cabin group was cohesive.' I'm not trying to pick on you, Jamie—just the opposite—you brought up a good example of something that wouldn't traditionally be thought of as a potential data point."

"I suppose that's true," Stu said. "Previously, we were thinking of the staff surveys mainly from a sort of damage control perspective. Hoping nobody felt unsupported or unprepared or anything."

"I remember taking them before Dan promoted me," Nico said. "It reminded me of the teaching effectiveness surveys we have to take at college. Those are all about outcomes, not about feelings."

"At the risk of sounding too much like a social worker, I'm going to recommend that we lean harder into feelings," Samira said.

"What's the camper survey like?" Maria asked.

"It's pretty small," Nico said. "They fill it out in the middle of all the chaos of packing up their stuff."

"Well, I trust we're not going to make them sit down for hours, but how short does it really have to be? What's on it?"

"'Do you feel like your counselors cared about you?' 'Did you find activities that you liked?' 'Did you get along with your cabin mates?'" Stu offered.

"I think we can dig deeper," Samira said. "I know kids can get real reflective if you give them the right questions."

"Yeah, I agree," Maria said. "It sounds like there's something promising there, but we can definitely ask more. We've got lots of time to think about this, so don't worry about it for the next meeting, but I'd like all of us to be thinking about new questions for each of the surveys. Whatever you think is most important, feel free to ask about your respective arenas, but I also want us to keep this theme of growth that we identified earlier in our minds. So, maybe there's more to dig into in that regard on these surveys."

"'Parents, do you feel like your kid grew as a person?'" Stu suggested. "'Counselors, do you feel like you learned new skills?' 'Campers, did you try something new this summer?'"

"Yeah, things like that," Maria said. "And, again, not for the next meeting, but I think it would be good to have the surveys done before camp starts, maybe by the end of staff training. That way they'll align with our broader goals for the summer. Does that sound doable?"

Everyone voiced their agreement.

"I'm grateful to all of you for being so open with these challenges," Maria continued. "Again, I feel like there's overlap. A little looser of an overlap than what we love about camping, but still, it's there. Most of us are getting at this notion of a camp identity, or a camp culture. Jamie and Laverne, the staff we hire is a massive part of our culture, I'd say even the most important part. Samira, the work you do is in large part about maintaining the camp culture, training staff and teaching campers how to relate to each other. Stu, the data in your surveys tells us whether the culture we're actively trying to create is working. I don't want to sound sappy, but each of us has a role to play in creating a new culture that allows Blue Trail to grow and thrive. I mean that 100 percent genuinely."

"It did sound sappy," Jamie said. "But I agree."

"Thank you," Maria said, laughing. "Does anyone have anything else to add before we move to our next agenda item?"

Maria waited several seconds before opening the floor to responses to her next question: Why do people keep coming back to Blue Trail? This discussion was shorter and, thankfully, free of fireworks. But Maria was a little perturbed by the fact that this question didn't take long to get through. Most everyone said something along the lines of "their friends are here," or "they had a good time with their counselors and the activities." It felt pretty superficial. At one point, Laverne, perhaps detecting Maria's desire for a more substantive conversation on the subject, asked Nico directly why he kept coming back to Blue Trail, since he was most recently an actual camper and counselor.

He smiled wanly. "I liked the idea of camp and I liked what Blue Trail had to offer more than I liked the idea of starting over somewhere else."

"This is news to me," James said, eyes wide. "You weren't really attached to Blue Trail?"

"I am now," Nico said. "But when I was younger, not particularly. I won't lie."

Jamie looked appalled that a Blue Trail lifer such as Nico had expressed such a distance from the place he lived and breathed, but Maria appreciated the honesty, if only because it further illuminated that the Blue Trail leadership team really didn't know why people kept coming back to Blue Trail. It was an issue.

"This is another place where deeper survey data would help us out," Maria said. "Right now we all have theories, but we do need to learn why the people who keep coming back are coming back. I'm going to dive into the data we do have and see if I can pick up any common themes, but this will be a point of emphasis for this coming summer—collecting good data."

Whether it was because the energy level in the meeting had sunk, or they'd already gotten at a lot of what was on the back end of the agenda (*What is your biggest worry about camp this summer? What is one specific action that you think would improve camp?*) the team breezed through the remaining items, even coming to a quick, if vague, consensus in response to Maria's final question, "What do you need from me this summer?"

"What we need from you is to tell us what you need from us," Laverne said.

"We had some issues with that in the past," Jamie added. "Sometimes the previous owner took on a little too much and would get burnt out, then let things slip, and we really didn't know his mental state until it was a bit too late."

"Just be clear," Stu said. "Don't be afraid to put stuff on us. Everyone here wants to see Blue Trail succeed, and we're excited to work with you."

Maria beamed. It was the perfect thing to hear to close out the meeting.

"Sounds great," Maria said. "I'll, um, certainly do that. And this is a very open question, and I'm all ears, always, so keep the suggestions coming. Does this same time work next week for another meeting where we can circle back on the loose threads from this one?"

There were a couple thumbs ups, a couple "yes's," and one "affirmative" from Stu.

"Excellent," Maria said. "I'll send out an email in a bit with the specific things that we need to be thinking about before next week. Thank you all so much for taking the time this evening. I can't wait for everything we're going to accomplish together. Goodnight, everyone."

One by one, the leadership team flashed her a smile, and their boxes winked out until Maria was staring at just her own face, elated and relaxed. She wished that she was still in the company of Robyn and Lane, taking this meeting from their kitchen table and could debrief it with them after she logged off. Maria felt more optimistic than ever that she could prove their investment worthwhile.

Discussion activity 4.1

Maria starts the discussion by modeling what she wants from the rest of the team. Great leaders are aware that every single action they take—or behavior they exhibit—is a model for somebody else. Too often, leaders feel like their team should pick up expectations from modeling alone, without the benefit of clearly communicated expectations.

Think: Why might leaders believe that simply modeling a desired behavior is enough to drive change within their team? What are the potential drawbacks of this assumption?

Personal Reflection: Reflect on your own leadership style and identify areas where you can strengthen the link between modeled behavior and clear communication of expectations.

Challenge: How can you as a leader effectively communicate expectations – alongside their modeled behavior – to ensure understanding, alignment and consistent implementation across the team?

Discussion activity 4.2

Stu's comment about accepting responsibility for solving the problem he brought up is often a rare behavior on teams. Too frequently, people suggest issues without taking responsibility for the solution. How can teams build a culture of ownership?

Consider: How does stating, "I'll take ownership," differ from simply sharing a problem? What impact does it have on accountability and team dynamics?

Personal Reflection: Assess your own tendency to take ownership and identify areas where you can strengthen the leadership quality of accepting responsibility for solving a problem that exists.

Consider: How can you encourage and empower your team members to take ownership of problems, ultimately fostering a more proactive and solution-oriented environment? How do you motivate yourself to take ownership of problems, even when the grind of the day-to-day interferes with bringing your best self to the work?

Discussion activity 4.3

In our work, we often come back to the thought-provoking statement about how the importance of a manager's peer team—often called the leadership or executive team—might even hold more significance than the team they directly lead.
Define: What do you think this statement means? How does it make you think differently about your work?

Think: Beyond the success of your individual team, what impact can a truly aligned and supportive leadership team have on the entire organization?

Discuss: Have there been times when siloed efforts or misalignment between teams in your organization have hindered progress? How could stronger communication and collaboration have prevented it?

Challenge: Imagine you could only control the success of the combined leadership team, not your individual unit. What key actions would you prioritize to optimize this team's effectiveness?

CHAPTER 5
TENSION VS. CONFLICT

MARIA wasn't sure where to stand on Jamie and Laverne's battle over what kind of skills were most desirable in new hires. Each day of the week in between their last meeting and this one, she convinced herself of a different stance. She had come out of last week's meeting aligning more with Jamie, thinking it was more important to hire people whose personalities more closely mirrored the Blue Trail culture, especially now.

The following day, however, she'd reconsidered, realizing that culture could be instilled in staff members who were willing to adapt to it. You couldn't teach someone how to lead tennis if they didn't come in knowing how to swing a racket, but you could get an expert tennis player to buy into the desire to coach kids up every day.

The next day, she had yet another epiphany. Blue Trail, to her knowledge, had never been a "sports camp"; kids who wanted to spend their summer competitively honing a specific skill were already going elsewhere. Blue Trail had traditionally been about fun and relationships, even if Maria felt that there was more room to add growth and leadership development.

On the other hand, it occurred to her that the simplest solution was probably the truest: The best way to enhance the quality of their activities was to hire quality instructors. It was one important way to actualize their mission—and their promise to parents—that the campers would grow. And, after all, the backbone of every camp day was the activities, which campers signed up for on the basis of interest, even passion. They owed it to the campers to hire staff who would further stoke those passions.

Maria had even tried using the questions she'd sent to the others to chew on before the next meeting. One of them, perhaps the most important one, she wasn't able to answer. "Which activities, if any, need a more dedicated specialist than they've had in the past?"

Laverne hadn't mentioned any specific activities that had been inadequately managed or instructed in the past few summers, and, although she was certain he was making this comment in jest, Maria agreed with Jamie's sentiment that it was entirely unnecessary to seek out varsity or collegiate athletes to teach each activity.

The other questions only heightened her indecision. "Should we prioritize hiring applicants with experience teaching, playing, or participating in one or more of the activities we offer?" Sure, in an ideal world, they'd get multiple applicants who were experts in every activity at Blue Trail, but clearly, they didn't, or else this wouldn't be an issue in the first place. Laverne simply didn't consistently have the people to make sure each activity was staffed by an expert.

Another thing that would be easier would be if we could keep counselors around for more than one summer, Maria thought.

She also respected Jamie's insight that the overall quality and camaraderie of the staff decreased when members didn't stay year after year. Maria would love it if they could get as many campers as possible to make the jump from camper to CIT, and then to counselor, but that had become difficult. So, in the turbulent era they were in, didn't it make more sense to seek out people who seemed like a better fit for Blue Trail, in the hopes that they'd be more inclined to stay on for additional summers?

Maria had started thinking about it along a binary of whether it was smarter to target keeping campers or keeping counselors. Offering more quality instruction could lead to more campers coming back to Blue Trail year after year with the hopes of genuinely gaining more skill in the activities they loved. Hiring Jamie's way, based more on personality and cabin counseling skills, could maintain or increase staff morale and competence. That would increase the chance of counselors staying on for multi-year careers (and make Jamie's off-season work a lot less stressful).

There were more campers, and campers were the ones bringing in money, so maintaining those ranks was harder and more important. But, at least at Starry Sky, campers often came back in part because of the actions of their favorite counselors, so would it be smarter to focus on having a consistently great staff? Maria knew this was probably a too simple way of thinking about it, but it helped organize her thoughts. She was desperate to know what the other members of her team were thinking.

She opened the video chat room right at the agreed-upon time. One by one, everyone's faces popped in on the screen.

"Hey there," Maria said. "How is everyone doing?"

"Good," Jamie said. "Ready to pick up where we left off."

Maria smiled. "All right, yes, me too. Anyone got anything fun to share from their non-camp lives?" Nobody took her up on the offer. She was, of course, curious about their lives, but today, she respected the fact that everyone wanted to get down to business.

"Hopefully everyone got my email with the agenda," Maria said regally. "It's just two items today, but they're pretty big, so I appreciate everyone being here and ready to discuss. First up: Stu, do you want to share your screen and talk about what you've brainstormed regarding what we talked about last week? The system for notifying you about campers' well-being more quickly?"

"Sure," Stu said. "Give me a moment." Maria could see computer windows sliding around in the reflection of his glasses. Finally, his screen appeared on hers. It was a pretty simple electronic form for an incident report, with blanks for camper name, the actual incident, the attending counselor, the response taken, and the time and day.

"This is part one and it's more of a revision to the system we have in place than any kind of revolutionary new idea," Stu explained. "We've been using paper incident reports and they just don't cut it if counselors don't bring their binders everywhere they go—and they don't, because why would you want one more thing to carry around and possibly forget someplace? And sometimes they forget to fill out a report when they get back to their cabin later, in which case a parent will call me when they get the 'unofficial' report in a letter from their kid, and they're rightfully peeved. So I made this electronic version."

"So counselors would use their phones to fill it out once everything is under control?" Maria asked.

"That's the idea," Stu said. "I know we've historically banned phone use in front of campers unless it's an emergency, but, well, these reports are urgent, so I'd support this slight increase in phone usage if it means I know about more accidents."

"I think that's reasonable," Jamie said.

"My only concern would be the Wi-Fi," Maria said. "Does camp get good reception? Or does the office Wi-Fi extend to everywhere that counselors could be?"

"The Wi-Fi is pretty good for the picnic area, near the athletic fields, and most of the cabins." Jamie said. "Reception is hit or miss."

"We'd still have paper backups," Stu said. "And my hope would be that allowing counselors to use their phones for this would make them more likely to remember to do it in any fashion, too. If their phone isn't working, maybe now they remember to go get their binder and fill out the report right away because they couldn't do it on their phone. It still won't be perfect, probably, but I think it will be a marked improvement."

"We'd still need the paper ones for trips anyway," Nico said.

"Very true," Stu said.

"Yeah, I definitely approve of this," Maria said. "Worthwhile phone usage, for sure."

"Amazing," Stu said. "Part two incoming in just a moment." He switched the window on his screen. A document with a massive table appeared. There were rows for camper names, and columns for specific actions that a counselor could, presumably, check off or leave blank.

"This is a bit more of an overhaul," he explained. "My thought was that counselors could fill this out with their campers each night, then run them over to me in the office the next morning. It's basic check-in stuff, mostly about their physical needs. Whether they showered that day, whether they wrote a letter home, whether the bodily plumbing is all in working order ... "

"You want a permanent record of whether kids pooped?" Laverne asked.

"I want a permanent record of whether they're eating enough and healthy," Stu said seriously. "This is a way of finding that out."

"I like it," Maria said. "I'm concerned that some campers would figure out why all this stuff is being asked and just lie if they felt like they needed to avoid scrutiny. Not saying that we shouldn't do this, just pointing it out."

"It will probably happen," Stu said. "But I'm not so worried about that, that's why we're having the counselors fill these out with the campers. They probably know the answers to all the questions, but they're using the campers to get answers to the ones they don't know, and then they pass the completed forms on to me so I have a record. That way, when parents call me, I can say with confidence that their kid is healthy, well-fed and happy. Or I can tell them specifically what we're seeing and what we're doing to address it."

"I wonder if this could be electronic, too," Nico said.

"I think this should stay on paper, unless you think the pileup of forms would be too much to manage, Stu," Maria said.

"I'd envisioned it as paper, but it could work either way. I'd honestly rather navigate a bunch of file folders than a nest of online folders and forms, though."

"We'll start out with paper and if it gets too unwieldy, we'll figure out a way to make the switch. But I think these are two great solutions. I really appreciate it."

"Of course," Stu said gallantly. "I appreciate you, all of you. Two meetings, and my job is already gonna be a lot easier."

It was time to move to the big ticket item on the agenda, the one Maria had been wrestling with all week. Even though Maria still wasn't perfectly clear which side of the debate she fell on, she did know that she wanted to foreground their discussion with some thoughts on how to disagree effectively.

"In a bit, we'll move on to the discussion of our hiring priorities. But I wanted to share some broader thoughts first," Maria said. The team looked at her expectantly. She took a moment to gather her words.

"I, personally, am not a fan of conflict," she began. "I don't think good team environments have conflict. Does anyone know why?"

"Because we should all be civil?" Nico guessed boredly.

"Ideally, yes," Maria said. "But that's not why. Anyone else?" Nobody felt like playing her guessing game, which was fine. "You might say this is just semantics, but look at the context in which the word 'conflict' is used outside of a professional setting. It's often literally geopolitical. Military. Two sides with completely opposite, mutually-exclusive goals. One side wants this bit of land that the other side is occupying. Or both sides need the resource and have entirely different uses for it. It's intractable. They are in conflict.

"Now, aside from the obvious fact that when people on a professional team disagree, nobody is bringing out tanks or guns or bombs, the definition of conflict still doesn't work. A good team doesn't have opposite goals. They have disagreement or tension on the best way to achieve the same goal. What is our goal?"

"To hire a staff full of people who can teach the activities at our camp," Laverne said.

"Or, to hire a staff that already exemplifies the Blue Trail way in their daily lives," Jamie said.

"Yes, but these are individual goals and I don't see them as mutually exclusive," Maria said. "Let me clarify and probe a little further. What is the larger goal that this disagreement is helping us build toward?"

"Hiring the best staff?" Jamie said.

"Even bigger," Maria said. "This whole disagreement, and all tension we'll have in the future as a leadership team, should be pushing us toward the goal of retaining 80% of campers and 60% of staff, and one strategy that we seemed to identify last week for doing this was helping people grow into leaders. I've been thinking about that all week. I thought it was really important that when asked about your favorite thing about camp, everyone came back to growth in some capacity. And what happens when people stay at camp for the full arc of a camping career?"

"They become a leader," Nico said. "They go from camper to CIT to counselor to unit head, and, in some cases," he spread his hands, motioning to the people on the call, "they go even higher."

"Do people agree with this goal?" Maria asked. "I think we should run with it as part of our main focus for the summer, but I'm curious for thoughts. Sorry, I guess this should've been part of the agenda, but I wanted to talk about the conflict-tension distinction before jumping into the hiring conversation."

"The goal rings true," Samira said. Everyone else agreed.

"I think the distinction between conflict and tension seems pretty semantic, though," Stu said. "Why do you see it as important to separate the two? For instance, do you not want us to say the word conflict?"

Maria chuckled. "No, I won't be that much of a stickler with the actual word. But I firmly believe in the idea that conflict is between groups or people with goals that are opposite of each other. And that just doesn't, or shouldn't, apply to teams that are working with each other toward the same overarching goal, rather than individual interest goals."

Maria hoped that the last bit hadn't sounded targeted. But it occurred to her that the reason Jamie and Laverne seemed so ready to lock horns over this issue was that the outcome stood to enhance or diminish each of their perceived contributions to Blue Trail. If they leaned harder into beefing up activities, people might give Laverne the credit. If they stayed the course, or put even more emphasis on hiring mainly for personality, it would benefit Jamie, who was already so popular among parents and staff.

"I wouldn't have made the distinction myself, but hey, words have precise definitions, or else we wouldn't have so dang many of them," Samira said, chuckling. "I can see that tension is probably more accurate to what we want here, and from my perspective, I definitely think it's a good call to work from the idea of engaging around tensions and helping people grow into leaders. The question then becomes whether we put the focus on the soft skills or the hard skills, for both campers and counselors. What are the qualities that help people become leaders?"

Those were Maria's thoughts exactly. Either route they took would conceivably help everyone grow. It was just about which qualities they thought were most important to develop, and which ones they thought a camp environment was best suited to nurture.

"When you put it like that, Samira, I think the soft skills seem more important," Jamie said. "You teach a kid how to play a sport, or a counselor how to teach a sport, then, great, they know that. But you help someone learn how to relate to other people, how to contribute to an environment that feels safe and supportive and happy ... that sticks with them everywhere they go down the line."

"Yeah, in theory, sure," Laverne said. "But what sense of accomplishment do they get during the summer, then?"

"What do you mean?"

"I mean, even if they feel safe and supported and all that—which, obviously, you want regardless –how are they getting the sense that they're growing?"

Maria was grateful that Laverne was already bringing in their larger goal, and her statement made her reconsider things yet again. After Samira spoke, Maria had been in agreement with Jamie. If you were to compare soft skills to hard skills, emotional intelligence versus technical competence, it seemed more important for people to be learning the former. But equally important, especially with their new pseudo-mission statement, was the ability for people to feel their growth over the course of a summer.

"I think that's a good point," Maria said. "Tangibility is important."

"Look at basketball, for instance," Laverne continued. "And basketball is normally one of our stronger activities, but still, it could be better. If the activity leader just puts everyone into a scrimmage, fine. It's fun for the kids, it's low maintenance for the counselor—as long as nobody gets hurt and everyone has a good time, it's a successful day and the kids who are really good at basketball already feel really accomplished. But there's not as much growth there. I understand that doing drills is a little groan-worthy for the campers, and it means the counselors have to step up and lead a thing even though they're already super drained, but in the end, it's going to be better for everyone.

"Say a kid comes into the week not really knowing anything about basketball. Can't dribble, can't shoot, nobody is going to pass to this kid in a game. Therefore, a game isn't going to help them grow. Doing drills every day, however, will not only help this kid develop skills, but the kid can then see their own growth when we point out that at the beginning of week they made two out of ten free throws, and at the end of the week they made seven."

"Is that a 'hiring different people' change?" Jamie asked. "Or could we just instruct the counselors to lean into teaching? Or teach them how to teach?"

"Yeah, we could," Laverne said. "But that's what I've been saying—they don't have the necessary skills to really help campers improve."

"Is that true, though?" Samira asked. "I mean, with respect, how intense of instruction are we really looking to impose? Sticking with the basketball example, this isn't a school team, it's not an NBA development academy. I think what Jamie said is important. We shouldn't be looking for people based on whether they know the most advanced plays or analytics or whatever. If we want to beef up activities, what we need to be doing is hiring people who are willing to do so, like Laverne said, even on the hard days."

This jogged an old lesson from Robyn and Lane in Maria's memory. The assets of any prospective hire could be sorted into three categories: knowledge, skills and dispositions. In a way, it was similar to Samira's dichotomy of soft skills and hard skills, but this was more specific. Knowledge referred to the facts, theories, and concepts that people learned through experience or training. Skills were the practical application of knowledge, the abilities and competencies gained through their experiences and acquisition of knowledge. And finally, dispositions are the attitudes, values, and personal qualities that influence how individuals approach situations, interact with others, and respond to challenges.

Maria laid out this framework for the team, thinking it could be useful for Jamie when making his hires and useful for them all to consider throughout staff training and the summer. The idea of knowledge, skills, and dispositions wasn't only useful when looking at who to hire, but when tracking the personal and professional development of others, as well as one's own. It was possible to grow and to expand one's capabilities in each of the three facets, even dispositions. People would always come into camp with their own personality, and often, they'd be hired based on that personality. But it was also possible for people to gain more positive dispositions through experience or training. Some desirable dispositions for camps included adaptability, perseverance, creativity, and a growth mindset. Maria had seen a lot of people come into Starry Sky lacking in some of the knowledge or skills that Laverne would think were required to lead an activity, but because they possessed these desirable dispositions, and they'd been continually asked back for multiple summers.

"So, what are you saying?" Laverne asked. "You don't need basketball skills to teach basketball?"

"You need some skills, absolutely," Maria said. "But, more importantly, you need to have the disposition to come back, day after day, and advocate for the importance of drills to a bunch of campers who are going to be whining at you to just let them play a game, instead. You need to have the disposition to do some research to fill in the blanks of your knowledge, to find new drills, to learn how to instruct certain things. You need to have the disposition to recognize, that in the end, keeping up with the instruction is going to be better for the campers because it will help them grow, and it'll be better for you because you are being a better and more engaged leader than you would've been if you had just sat back, let them scrimmage, and made sure nobody dislocated a shoulder."

"So then it sounds like the improvement spot might not be the hiring," Samira said. "It might be staff training."

"Maybe so," Maria said. "How much time do we spend on activities in staff training?"

"Not a ton," Jamie said. "We give the activity heads time to plan out what they're going to do for the first week. The things we go over as a whole staff are mostly just safety protocols."

"I think this year that should change," Maria said. "Laverne, are you satisfied with this? Does this resonate with you, the idea of pushing activity heads harder to come up with instruction, rather than hiring too differently?"

Laverne looked deep in thought. Maria understood what was probably going through her mind. She'd invested a lot of mental energy in the tension with Jamie and this didn't feel like a total win. But hopefully it would help accomplish the larger goal and Maria hoped that Laverne would see that.

"If this is what the group thinks is best, I'll support it," Laverne said gruffly. "I'm not entirely sold on the idea that it's all disposition. I feel like I've tried to get people to instruct more and it doesn't work, because they just might not have the knowledge and skills. But that's always been a mid-summer adjustment. Maybe it would go differently if we were blowing this horn from the beginning of staff training."

"I think it would," Maria said. "It's hard to ask people to make a big pivot in their approach in the middle of the summer, when they've settled into a groove and they're tired from everything else they have to do on a daily basis and they're not being supervised every day to make sure they're doing it. If things are going to change, it's going to start at staff training, and that would probably be true even if we hired a bunch of elite instructors."

See discussion activity 5.1 at the end of the chapter

"Yeah, I can agree with that," Laverne said.

"Okay," Maria said. "Unless anyone else is opposed, I say we keep hiring the way Jamie sees fit, and we bring more emphasis on instruction into staff training. Sound good?"

"Sounds good," Jamie said. Laverne smiled thinly at his chipper response, but voiced her agreement as well. As did everyone else.

There was nothing else on the agenda and they'd wrapped up this discussion much faster than Maria had anticipated. She was pleased at the way everyone had come together. It hadn't gotten as heated as the last meeting, she'd gotten to express some of the theories and teachings she'd inherited from Robyn and Lane, and the team had solved the issue at hand. Or, at least, they had agreed on a solution that she was optimistic about for next summer.

But, more importantly, Blue Trail had a goal. An official goal. One that they all knew needed to be met, yet had gone unspoken just the same. It was now their focus to retain more campers and staff year in and year out. And today was yet another step in helping the camp culture grow, so that everyone who was a part of the Blue Trail community wanted to stay a part of it.

Discussion activity 5.1

Beyond the Learning Burst:

Think: Reflect on past professional development experiences. What stuck with you? What faded away? Why?

Discuss: How do learned skills or knowledge from training days struggle to translate into daily practice within your team or organization? What were the barriers?

Challenge: Imagine a year from now. You want to remember your professional development days not just as a day off, but as a catalyst for positive change. What needs to happen between now and then?

Personal Responsibility: Reflect on your own role in driving continuous learning and the change that follows. What can you do to hold yourself and others accountable for implementing change and seeking new knowledge?

CHAPTER 6

SAMIRA'S ASK

A COUPLE weeks later, Maria found herself at a large hotel in Denver. She was clutching a to-go cup of coffee and watching the elevators go up and down through the cavernous atrium, waiting for her team members to step out of the doors.

This year's American Camp Association National Conference was in Denver, which ironically, was less than two hours from Starry Sky, and she was glad she'd been able to fly in the leadership team on such short notice. The dates had snuck up on her this year, in the midst of everything else she had to navigate about the transition. She hadn't attended the conference every year she'd been on the leadership team at Starry Sky, because Robyn and Lane, despite getting a lot out of the conference each year they went, never made it mandatory for the rest of the team. In the last few years, something had always come up the week of the conference that prevented Maria from going. There had even been a rare February wedding in her family. A small ceremony, unsurprisingly.

The American Camp Association conference was apparently much more of an institution among the Blue Trail leadership team. Jamie had emailed her shortly after their previous meeting, "Just wanting to confirm whether we were still going to be in attendance at the ACA conference." Maria didn't remember ever mentioning anything about the conference, even when they met all those months ago when she first visited Blue Trail.

But, even on such short notice, everyone on the team was here. Nico said he could skip a few days worth of classes from his senior year of college. Jamie and Maria didn't have other jobs, with both of their camp jobs having enough off-season responsibilities to merit relatively fulsome salaries. Stu worked as a delivery driver to supplement his camp salary, so he could set his own schedule. Even Laverne, who, out of everyone, Maria figured was the most likely to use short notice as an excuse to sit out the event, had replied brusquely but affirmatively to Maria's email invitation, saying "It'll work fine, I haven't used my personal days yet." Samira dipped into her time off, as well. The conference really did seem to matter to everyone at Blue Trail.

Maria had used camp funds to purchase plane tickets, and while she grimaced at the inflated, two-weeks-out prices, she knew that it would be worth it. The conference offered valuable networking opportunities and the chance to absorb new ideas and advice from those who knew the camping world best. There would be seminars and talks hosted by experts in anything you could ever hope to learn about camp operations, including leadership and child development. And it would be a good chance for the new Blue Trail team to bond before the summer actually started.

Maria had noticed that the atrium of this conference hotel resembled a gigantic ribcage. Elevators zipping up and down the spine, the tan plaster floors curving outward like bones. It all felt a little too grand for a group of people who spent their summers sleeping in wooden cabins and walking around in the dirt. Maria sipped her coffee. It was noticeably better than what she'd drank each morning in the dining hall at Starry Sky.

The elevators were made of glass and she'd been staring inside them for minutes now, trying to make out the figure of one of her team members, but they were too far away. It therefore surprised her when Samira's voice rang out, "Hey, what are you staring at?"

Maria was grateful there was a lid on her coffee cup. She scanned the walkway in front of her and quickly saw Samira walking towards her. She smiled and embraced her when they met.

"Glad to see you," Maria said.

"You, too."

"Have you seen any of the others yet?"

"They'll be down soon, I'm sure," Samira said. "They don't know how weird you get about punctuality."

"I'm not weird, it's just not that hard. Besides, they're not late yet."

"Yeah, you're not weird," Samira replied with a smirk.

"That didn't sound genuine."

They didn't have to wait long. Nico popped out of the elevator a minute later, then Stu, Laverne, and lastly, Jamie. The leadership team's streak of on-time arrivals to meetings and meet-ups remained unbroken.

"I'm so glad we're all here!" Maria said. "Thank you all for making the trip on such short notice."

"Of course," Jamie said.

"First time here," Nico said. "I'm excited. Never been to a better party."

Samira laughed.

"Has everyone looked at the day's schedule?" Maria asked. Everyone had indeed perused. "Obviously people are welcome to hit the same panels, but feel free to spread out as well, when we reconvene at the end of the day, I want us to be able to talk about a lot of different things."

"Should we be sticking to stuff that's close to our job descriptions?" Samira asked.

"I don't think we have to, necessarily," Maria said. "It would probably be useful to go to a few that talk about stuff each of us ourselves could implement, but we're all camping world aficionados. I trust that we'd each have the ability to share out about any panel in this building. Were you eyeing one in particular?"

"Not really," Samira said. "Just curious." It was perhaps the first time ever that Maria was suspicious that Samira wasn't telling the truth.

"There's one that's literally called 'Programming for Pennies,'" Laverne said. "Could be up our alley at this point."

"I can't disagree," Maria said. "Anyone else see anything great?"

"'The Art of Hard Conversations' at 11 a.m.," Stu said. "That's my job, a lot of the time."

"Same here," Samira said. "Maybe I'll join you."

"Those sound awesome," Maria said. "There was only one that I thought we should all go to, it's on goal setting and evaluation at 4:30."

Everyone said that it fit with what they had planned for the day and they went their separate ways, some to an early event, others to grab some coffee. Maria would be heading to a meetup for new directors and directors in new places in a bit. She still had some time before that, though, so she headed over to a pod of comfortable-looking green chairs and sat down. To her surprise, Samira followed her.

"Can we talk for a moment?" Samira said.

"Yeah, of course."

Samira sat down across from her. She'd been wearing a small leather backpack and she set it down to the side of her chair. Her hands were clasped, her elbows on her knees.

"So, I recognize that this may not be a great time and I could've brought this up before we got here, but I wanted to follow up on what we sort of talked about when we discussed challenges a couple weeks ago."

"Oh, gosh," Maria said. "Yeah, let's talk right now."

Every word Samira had said when she'd shared out came rushing back to her now. And Maria had promised that they could talk privately and then never reached out. She remembered being so curious about what Samira was really feeling and a little worried that she'd only said yes to switching camps because she hadn't wanted to disappoint Maria. She couldn't believe she'd forgotten to follow up.

"So, let me dispel a couple of things I imagine you're worried about right away," Samira said. Maria smiled, grateful for their familiarity. Any other employee probably wouldn't start a conversation with their ostensible superior this way. "I came to Blue Trail to do exactly the job I did at Starry Sky, just like you proposed. So this isn't me throwing in some late stage ultimatum. I'm not planning on going anywhere."

"I'm glad to hear that," Maria said.

"But, as I alluded to in the meeting a couple weeks ago, I feel like I could be doing more. I want to be doing more. I feel comfortable in my responsibilities as a social worker, I like helping kids process their emotions and I like helping counselors be more thoughtful leaders. But, sometimes, it feels like the least camp-y job in camp. Aside from my emotions — "

"I do care about your emotions, though," Maria said.

"Thank you," Samira said. "But aside from that, I think it would make sense for me to do some more supervision of counselors, activity leaders, maybe the CITs, especially. I don't know whether Jamie handles that, or you, but I want to be a more visible resource. It would be more fulfilling for me, but more importantly, it would allow people to talk to me before things become a crisis. And, eventually, it could make sense for me to be a part of the hiring process, as well. Another way of looking at the position of social worker is like that of a 'culture czar,' so having me screening for compatible dispositions at the start would be helpful. Those are two responsibilities I thought of, but I'm open to doing anything else you think of as well,"

It sounded to Maria like Samira was angling for the position, or at least, the responsibilities of assistant director. It wasn't uncommon for camps to have multiple assistant directors, especially when they only had one director.

"The supervision idea makes a lot of sense," Maria said. "I mean, I'm not exactly sure who supervises activities right now, other than Laverne, but I know I'd like to be sitting in on them from time to time as well. Me, you, and Jamie all could."

Something didn't feel quite right to Maria. Out of the three she mentioned, Samira honestly seemed like the odd one out for that particular responsibility. But she wouldn't be, if she was promoted.

Samira, as she so often did, knew what Maria was thinking. "If I do what I did at Starry Sky, then I'll be the one leading a lot of the professional development that the counselors will use during their activity leading, anyway. Wouldn't it also make sense for me to supervise, to make sure it's being implemented correctly?" Samira asked.

"No, it does make sense, you're right," Maria said.

"You sound hesitant," Samira said, smiling.

"I'm not hesitant."

"Maria."

"Okay, I'm a little hesitant. You came with me from Starry Sky, I'm worried that giving you a bunch of extra responsibilities that the others have handled for years would be perceived as favoritism."

"Sure, but when does the statute of limitations on that policy expire?"

"I don't know, not immediately." Maria was wishing Samira had brought this to her before signing on at Blue Trail. Then she could've introduced her as someone who was going to help out with these additional responsibilities. If she wasn't concerned about appearances, she would, of course, promote Samira. There was no question about whether Samira was qualified.

"Okay, well, from my perspective, it doesn't make sense for one person to handle all the supervision and especially for just one person to have all the hiring power," Samira said. "Look at my school, for example. The vice principal and I both observe teachers. We work together to make sure that all of the teachers get feedback and we each fill in the areas that the other isn't as well-equipped to supervise. Laverne and I could both observe activities, just looking for different things. Same deal with hiring. I trust Jamie's idea of a good disposition, a hirable disposition. Then again, we can't retain staff ..."

"I don't think that's all on Jamie," Maria said, surprised Samira would throw shade on him so directly. "Staff members are coming into camp expecting one thing and getting another." Maria scanned their surroundings and lowered her voice before continuing. It probably wasn't a great idea to go on a tangent of criticizing her own camp at a conference full of people from other camps. "Blue Trail's had an amazing reputation for decades and something that the camp as a whole has been doing the last several years has created a gap between expectation and reality. We've stagnated. That's not all on one person."

"You're right," Samira said. "That was petty of me."

"It's okay," Maria said. "You were saying?"

"I still think more than one person should be involved with the hiring. What was it like at Starry Sky?"

"By my last summer there, it was basically a team effort between me, Robyn, and Lane. They started me out just conducting some interviews and eventually had me going through applications with them, as well."

"See? It's not just one person, not even just the director."

Maria chuckled. "I thought they'd involved me because they were training me to be the director. I guess they were, just not at Starry Sky."

"I'm guessing it was also because they didn't want the rest of the leadership team waiting 'til day one of staff training to learn who would be taking care of the campers the whole summer!" Samira said, spreading her hands.

That got a full laugh. "Okay, true. Sounds like I should be assisting Jamie with this, then, not you," she joked. Samira rolled her eyes. "Relax, I'm kidding." She wondered if Dan, the previous Blue Trail director, had also been hands-off during the recruitment and hiring process.

"It's not a zero sum game," Samira said. "If I help with observation, I'm not taking Laverne's job, she's still doing that job. If I help with hiring, it's still Jamie's responsibility. The only way you'd be perceived as playing favorites is if you literally took responsibilities from them, or fired them and had me take over. But that's not what's gonna happen and it's certainly not what I'm asking for."

Maria supposed it was common for responsibilities to overlap. The worries with that style of leadership would be inefficiency, and potentially overburdening someone. But, at this point in Blue Trail's history, Maria could see the argument for more teamwork. The camp wasn't in a place where it could just hum along with individuals simply completing their individual responsibilities.

"All right," Maria said. "You'll supervise activities with Laverne, coordinating your schedules so you each go to every activity once per week. I think it'd be wise not to do it on the same day, just so the activity leaders don't feel too much like they're on trial."

"That sounds great to me," Samira said. "Four activity periods per day, right? How many activities do we have?"

"I'm not sure of the exact number. Less than twenty. Once per week should work and if not, we'll roll with it. And I want to table the hiring idea until the end of summer, but I'm very open to it. I think you make a great point that there shouldn't be just one person in charge of finding a whole staff, both for the camp's sake and for that person's sake. But I don't want to make anything official on that front yet."

"Yeah, I understand," Samira said. "It's a more drastic change than me observing some activities, for sure."

"In the meantime, though, I think it'd be good if you took on a more front-facing role in staff training," Maria said. "If you're down. You're right – you're the one who's going to be touching base with the staff most about their progress over the course of the summer. It makes sense for you to be on stage, so to speak, right at the beginning of their journey. And you're a good speaker. You do know what you're talking about. You want to be more of a visible presence? That could be a good place to start."

"I agree. I'll take on whatever parts of training you think suit me," Samira said.

"You can do even more than that. I think we're going to be tinkering a lot with how Blue Trail does staff training. But we'll need your input especially. If you have things you want broadcasted that haven't historically been on the agenda, you should bring it to us, and then you should definitely be the one to lead it during training."

"I will," Samira said. "I really appreciate you taking this so seriously."

"I'm glad you want to take on more," Maria said. "You deserve to, you deserve to have this transition be more than a lateral move for you, if that's what you want."

"Like I said, I would've been happy just to get the chance to build something new with you at Blue Trail. But I'm very happy to do more. I feel ready."

"You're definitely ready." Maria checked her phone. "How much longer until your first session?"

"Not long," Samira said, peering over at the time. "Ten minutes or so."

"If I had put up more of a fight, you might've missed it."

"I would've had to excuse myself, yes," Samira said. "It's on camper-on-camper bullying, I always want to know the best practices for addressing that, for both sides. How do I get at the root cause? How do I give the one who's being picked on the courage to solve their own issues while also providing adequate support?"

"Yeah, that's an important one," Maria said. "I'll look forward to hearing more later."

"It'll be nice to debrief. Maybe we should all go out for dinner," Samira said.

"I think that's a great idea. I'll look for a nice place. It can be on me. No more dipping into the camp budget for this trip."

Samira laughed. "Shrewd move." She stood, swinging her backpack onto one shoulder. "I'll see you later! Thank you again, so much."

"Of course, anytime. Enjoy the day."

Samira walked away, surprisingly quiet against the polished floor. Maria picked up her phone to study the day's schedule once more, seeing if there were any sessions she'd missed on her first several glances that would be worth attending.

CHAPTER 7

TEAM DINNER

THE host showed them to a high-top table beneath a long, spindly chandelier. The restaurant was all clean lines and hard accents, and Maria observed the contrast between this and the pictures she'd seen of Blue Trail's dining hall, which was bathed in warm wood tones and clad with pictures of past summers.

The Mess Hall at Starry Sky had always been Maria's favorite place to eat. The simple act of sitting down on one of the long benches—be it with her cabin as a camper and counselor, or at the directors' table once she'd joined the leadership team—for the first time in a given summer always felt like the official start of camp. Even when the campers had already arrived, it didn't feel like summer had really begun until everyone was sitting down tucking into their meal together. Maria hoped she'd feel that same feeling of home at Blue Trail's first dinner. For now, she was feeling more and more comfortable with the leadership team, even if their current environs were quite different from a camp meal. They all deserved a nice night out on the town.

A waiter came to take drink orders and everyone stuck with water. When the waiter retreated, Maria kicked off the conversation.

"How'd everyone feel about today?" she said.

"The programming talk I went to was great," Laverne said. "I got lots of ideas for evening activities, especially ones that don't involve just running around. I think we could stand to do a little less capture the flag style stuff and some more creative things."

"Yeah?" Maria said. "Were there any specific thoughts that came to you right away?"

"I wrote a bunch down," Laverne responded. "The one that immediately sprang to mind was a talent show for counselors, or groups of campers. The ideas are less important than the logic, I think, but obviously I'm grateful for the ideas. I'll give y'all the list. Every summer I've noticed that there's always a clique of campers who don't really care for the evening activity and I think that's because a lot of the ones we normally do are just more athletic stuff. Or an additional structured free period."

At Starry Sky, they'd prided themselves on having a diverse and creative array of evening programming and a lot of those ideas had come from counselors. This was an area where Maria felt they could make an immediate and positive change this summer.

"That sounds great," Maria said. "I'd love to see that list and I don't know whether Blue Trail has done this in the past, but at least in my experience, counselors are often really eager to contribute ideas for evening activities when you invite them to take a leadership role."

"We'd love for counselors to come up with programs," Jamie said. "I feel like they used to bring us ideas all the time and then in the last few years that stream of ideas has slowed to a trickle. Or a drip-drop. Nothing really."

"Do you have any guesses as to why the stream of ideas has slowed down over time?" Maria asked.

"We always ask for ideas when we talk about evening activities during staff training," Stu said. "I think we've advertised it with pretty much the same fervor for the last several years, but Jamie's correct, there's been less pickup in the last few."

"It all comes back to staff culture," Maria said. "It's like you said a while back, Jamie, if the staff doesn't gel as much with each other anymore, they're not going to feel as comfortable creating and collaborating with each other, and if they're not feeling like they can be creative, or feeling motivated to push themselves to come up with new things, they won't feel as much drive to come back summer after summer. They need those big moments where they feel like the kids are having fun because of something they created, whether that's a five-minute game played in their cabins, an activity they lead, or an all camp program."

"Well, let's push it harder during staff training, then," Jamie said with a laugh. "Evening activity ideas, come one, come all."

"I went to a talk on non-confrontational language," Samira said.

Stu mm-hmmed and Jamie nodded firmly.

"We talk a lot about it at my off-season work," Samira continued. "But I'm always curious about the application in a camp setting, where I feel like there can be even more in-your-face confrontation than in a school. Kids fight over games, over space, cabin habits, cliques. And it's really easy for counselors to get drained and focus on resolving conflicts as quickly and firmly as possible and end up using language and tone that comes across as really harsh and invalidating."

"That is the single most common thing I have to talk to counselors about," Jamie said. "I'll overhear someone trying to resolve a conflict between campers, and, like you put it, Samira, the language and the tone just aren't right. Even if they did come to a resolution to the actual problem."

Maria couldn't help but remember the argument between him and Laverne in the offseason. Although they'd come to a productive resolution as a team, the memory still made her question the nature of Jamie's relationship to feedback.

"Do you find that counselors are receptive when you step in?" Maria asked.

"Usually," Jamie said. "And I always try to model non-confrontational language when I have to talk to a counselor, too. 'I noticed that . . .'; 'I appreciate your effort...'; 'Can we talk about how to improve?' I think they see it as fake when it comes from me, or another supervisor. And then, for them, it's hard to fall back on it in the heat of a given moment."

"It's ironic," Maria said. "My sense is that people don't trust non-confrontational language because they can't shake the feeling that it is still confrontation. And they don't like confrontation. When it's a counselor and a supervisor, or a counselor and another counselor, they're afraid of it. And when it's a counselor and a camper, the counselor wants it resolved as fast as possible."

"But didn't you say you don't like conflict?" Nico asked. "Are conflict and confrontation different?"

"You're right," Maria said. "I don't like either of those things, I don't think either of them are part of a productive and trusting team. As I said before, I think non-confrontational language is a part of engaging around tension, which is a better phrase to describe what needs to happen when two people are at odds within a team with the same overarching goal."

Their waiter emerged again to bring a breadbasket and ask about any other appetizers. Nobody had even looked at the menu yet; they dove into their conversation so quickly. Maria felt a little bad bringing work into this lovely dinner, but she wanted to discuss the goal setting and evaluation talk they'd all attended. After that, if no one else had anything, they could order a round of drinks or desserts and talk about all the non-camp-related things she was genuinely curious to know about her coworkers.

She knew very little about anyone on her team except for Samira. Laverne had kids who had long since aged out of camp. Stu had mentioned a partner, but Maria didn't even know whether they came to camp together each summer. Nico was in college in California, but what was he studying? She guessed it was outdoorsy — environmental science or geology or something — but she ought to know. Maria asked the waiter for a minute and gave everyone time to decide what they wanted to eat. They ordered when the waiter returned and Maria picked up where they left off.

"This non-confrontational language stuff sort of brings me to what I wanted to bring up from the day," she said. "How'd we feel about that last panel?"

Maria had given the team leave to attend any talks they felt would be helpful to their individual arenas, but she had also asked everyone to go with her to one panel toward the end of the day. Two local business executives had lectured on a model of goal setting and evaluation that they had invented themselves. Though Maria tried to seek out panels led by people with strong connections to the camping world, this was the only talk related to goal setting that she saw on the schedule. She figured it would be better than nothing and it would at least give them some food for thought.

As it turned out, she had been right to be skeptical. The model sounded good, but that was the issue; the presenters hadn't made much of an effort to connect the buzzwords into actionable items for a camp. The few examples they gave were from their own business, and though Maria could see how it had helped them, very few people in the audience seemed ready to take it on as their camp's new guiding star. She found herself hoping someone on Blue Trail's leadership team would say that it had resonated more than expected, not only because she wanted a good model of goal setting to take into the summer, but frankly, because she felt bad making everyone show up to a milquetoast panel.

"Honestly?" Laverne asked.

Maria nodded, dreading the answer.

"Didn't feel great," Laverne said. "I don't know what those guys were doing at a camping conference."

Nico smacked his lips. "Lotta words. A lot of words."

"I can see what they were trying to get at, but, yeah—I'm having trouble seeing the forest for the trees, so to speak," Stu said, more elegantly.

"Jamie?" Maria asked.

He laughed. "Yeah, I agree with everyone else. Let's not

get too down in the dumps about it. It was just one panel."

"The subject is still important, though," Maria said. "I'd love to brainstorm something that works for us, if we don't feel like we can use their model."

"I'm not so sure we can't use it," Samira said. She was looking eagerly at Maria. "Sounds like I'm in the minority, but I can see the connections to camp. I'd love to share, if you all are open to hearing."

"I don't mean to kick the can, but maybe we get some dinner in our system first? It's been a long day," Jamie suggested.

This triggered smirks from Laverne and Nico, but they seemed to be tickled at his suggestion, not at Samira's initiative. Maria took that as a signal to push forward.

"I hear that," Maria said. "I'm hungry too, but we're all here, and we'll all be eating soon. I'd like to hear what Samira has to say." She didn't feel like that should've had to be said. Jamie's face turned a shade paler.

"Why not?" Nico said. "Bonus dinner panel."

"Bonus dinner panel, sure," Samira said. She plucked her bag off the back of her chair and retrieved her notebook and the blue ballpoint pen she'd been using to take notes all day. She opened a new page right after her notes from the panel and sketched four triangles; three surrounding one in the center.

"Yeah, this looks less complex already," Laverne said, and Maria laughed despite herself.

Once she was finished sketching, Samira twirled her pen to rest in her palm and looked up at the team.

"All right, so we had four essential components of teams that can successfully accomplish goals," Samira said. "Number one: focus.

"Focus means that everyone on the team agrees on their goal, works collaboratively toward that goal by using an agreed upon plan, adapts to challenges that arise, and pays attention to the results of their efforts," Samira continued, scribbling down some short bullet points in the focus triangle. "For us, that goal, which we agreed on, is helping campers grow, and helping counselors grow into leaders. We all work together toward that goal by providing challenging activities, by training counselors in leadership skills and conflict resolution."

"Tension engagement," Nico corrected.

Samira and Maria both chuckled. "Yes, tension engagement," Samira continued. "We also loop parents in on their kids' individual wins, big and small. We pay attention to campers emotional health and help them create relationships that they might not reach for on their own. We create a physically and emotionally safe environment for everyone at camp. We do all of this with one focus: to help people grow. This can be as big as helping a counselor develop more front-of-the-room charisma, or as granular as helping a kid make more free throws."

Samira wrote down the latter example on the paper. "Does everyone feel good about this part of the triangle?"

There were no objections. Everyone's eyes were on either Samira or the paper. Nobody looked as disinterested as they were during the panel. Whether that was because they didn't want to hurt the newest team member, or because Samira was explaining it in a truly more comprehensible way, Maria wasn't quite sure, but Samira pressed on, nonetheless.

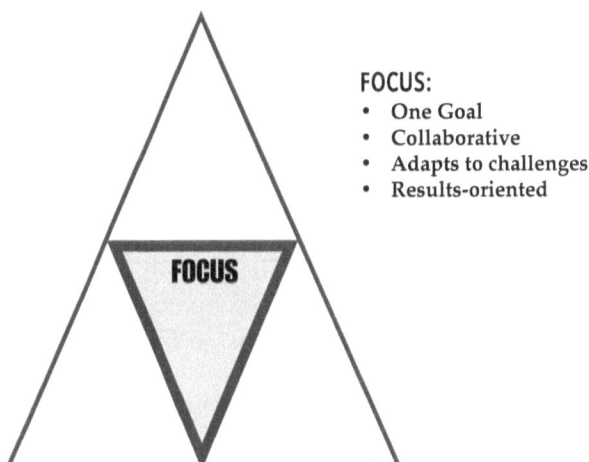

FOCUS:
- **One Goal**
- **Collaborative**
- **Adapts to challenges**
- **Results-oriented**

"Triangle number two is accountability," Samira continued, writing it down in the bottom middle corner of the pyramid. "This is a word that gets thrown around a lot, but effectively put into practice much less often. On paper . . ."

Stu laughed. "On paper," he repeated, motioning to the notebook.

Maria smiled. Puns meant people weren't zoning out.

"On paper," Samira repeated again, "good accountability means that, one, I do what I say I'm going to do; two, you do what you say you're going to do; and three, we all help each other do what we're supposed to do to meet our goals. If one of us doesn't live up to the expectations we've set for one another, we take it upon ourselves to call them in for an opportunity to grow and make it right."

"Maybe a dumb question," Nico said. "But are expectations the same as goals? Like, are we expecting to 'help people grow' this summer?"

"Maria?" Samira prompted. "Do you want to speak to that?"

"Sure. Definitely not a dumb question," Maria said. "Expectations, as I understand them, are more like responsibilities. Personal and team benchmarks. For you, that might be getting a certain percentage of younger campers to take a trip, you mentioned that as a goal going into this summer. Goals come with expectations that people should fulfill in order to meet them. We all believe that trips are a growth accelerant for campers, and our goal is for campers to grow, so our expectation is that more younger campers will go on trips this summer. And if that expectation doesn't end up being met, it would fall to you, as trips director, to find a new path toward meeting it or, with this team's agreement, adjusting it. Does that make sense?"

"Yeah," Nico said, grinning slightly. "Sounding less buzzword-y already."

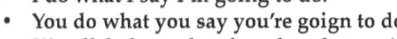
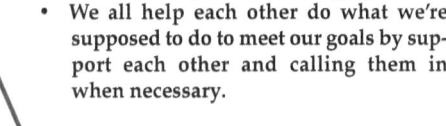

ACCOUNTABILITY:
* I do what I say I'm going to do.
* You do what you say you're goign to do.
* We all help each other do what we're supposed to do to meet our goals by support each other and calling them in when necessary.

There were now two sections of the triangle filled out. The page was becoming more full, and in Maria's mind it was starting to come together in a meaningful way.

"I'll type this all up nicely and send it to you all later," Samira said, pressing on cheerily. "There's more to add under each corner, but for now, corner number three! Communication. There are three kinds of communication that happen on high performing teams. Relational communication, task communication, and growth communication." She wrote them down on the bottom right triangle of the diagram. "Relational communication is the fun part. That's trust building, empathy, collaboration—all the stuff that builds team chemistry and makes people go from coworkers to friends."

Maria wrote a bullet in the bottom right triangle.

"One might say that this dinner is relational communication, then," Stu said.

"That makes it sound so clinical," Laverne offered.

"Maria, did you arrange this just to accomplish some relational communication?" Nico asked, deadpan.

"You got me," Maria joked. "But, in all seriousness, we want people on our staff to be friends. We talked about this a while back. Jamie, you've seen camaraderie appear to decrease. What can we do, as staff, to encourage communication that isn't just about work?"

"Staff talent show," Nico said immediately.

"The evening activity idea?" Laverne said.

"No, have it during staff training. Let people goof off on stage. By themselves or in groups. Or have other games. Lunches, team dinners. Anything. But, yeah, clearly our default mode of, I don't know, vibe setting isn't working, and we need to be a little more active in getting people to gel."

"That talent show idea sounds amazing, I think people would really love it," Samira said. "Maybe the last day of staff training."

"The last day would feel like a nice culmination," Maria said. "Another idea would be to do it mid-week. Then people would really feel the difference in how close they are to each other between the beginning of the week and the end. Either way, I think we work it into the schedule for sure." Everyone else nodded enthusiastically.

"Awesome idea, Nico," Samira continued. "Next up in this triangle is task communication. This is the nitty-gritty of work stuff. Communicating information, delegating, organizing, executing. A unit head bringing the other counselors up to speed on a unit field trip. A senior counselor assigning cleanup chores. Maybe even what we're doing now. It may sound like the most clinical, the least emotional, but I've found that it's surprisingly easy for people to struggle in this arena."

"Yeah, weirdly enough, when I observe activity leaders, this is the thing that trips them up the most," Laverne said. "Their energy is usually great,. but they're young. During the year, they're not used to being at the front of a room. I've seen way too many counselors get tripped up explaining the plan for the day or week to the rest of their team."

"Yeah, it's a thing. They have to grow into it," Maria said, trying to be gentle toward the teenagers Laverne was talking about. "But, yeah, no kid likes unclear rules. No counselor likes unclear expectations. None of us like being left in the dark. It's best to err on the side of overcommunication."

"Absolutely," Stu said. "Brings me back to the alert systems we created a few weeks back. One time a camper got a black eye—not from a fight or anything, just from running into another camper during a game—and the counselor gave him some ice. The bruise resolved itself in a couple days. But the kid thought it was cool that he got a black eye, told his mom and I got an angry phone call. And I didn't know what to say, because I hadn't been told anything; nobody thought it was a big deal."

"It shouldn't have been," Laverne said wryly.

"If it were my kid, yeah, I agree," Stu said. "But I don't know what the kid said in the letter to his mom and every parent is different. Every kid is different. Every counselor is different. People need different levels of support and communication. So I totally agree. Communicate proactively." He grabbed a roll and scooped out a generous glob of butter with his knife.

"We had plenty of stories like that at Starry Sky, too," Maria said, snatching a roll and some butter. The roll was warm and soft and fulfilling, far better than the soggy wrap the conference had provided for lunch. "There are always going to be frustrated parents and it's a good thing we have someone as great as you as our liaison. In the end, they all just want to know their child is safe and having fun."

"Everyone feeling good about task communication?" Samira asked. Everyone nodded. She continued on, writing more in the communication triangle. "Growth communication is aimed at personal or team development, goal setting, idea sharing, et cetera. The kind of communication that pushes the team forward toward further aspirations. This could be a whole other conversation, seeing as growth is our big goal for this summer and beyond, but for now, I'll write down that for growth communication to be effective, it needs to be supportive, non-judgmental, and specific.

"I'm thinking mainly of feedback here, Samira continued.

"Abstract feedback can be some of the most frustrating for our counselors, especially CITs. 'My senior counselor told me I need to be nicer to the kids.' Well, what does that mean? What behaviors are you observing and what should I be doing instead? Now I feel paranoid that I've been a bad counselor for weeks, the kids hate me, and my bosses hate me.

"When the growth communication is good, I imagine the rest of the triangle is a lot easier to hold together," Samira finished. "Again, we could spend days talking about this. But I know we will. And we're not the only ones who need to be in on this discussion."

"Not to diminish—if anything, just the opposite—but we talk about how to give feedback every summer," Jamie said. "I feel like, as a leadership team, we're pretty on top of observing our staff and guiding them in the right direction if they're doing stuff that doesn't fit with our vibe. And yet, they don't feel like they're growing. So I guess we're doing something wrong."

"I think that's an important thing to note, Jamie," Maria said. It was one of just a couple times she had seen Jamie admit vulnerability or weakness and she wanted to applaud it.

"Growth communication is really hard to get right. If you're too direct, some people take it as harsh. If you dance around trying to find the right words, people see you as fake. If you give too much feedback, people feel surveilled; if you give too little, your workplace suffers. And when you're working with people as young as our staff are, it gets even more delicate. But it's so important that we keep talking about this, keep training ourselves and our staff, so that everyone feels like they can develop, be creative, and be a part of achieving something. It sounds lofty, but it's real."

"Don't worry," Jamie said. "We're sold on the importance. It's just a delicate thing, as you say."

"We could do some feedback roleplay in staff training," Samira suggested. "Run through some common scenarios. It would give counselors a chance to practice, give us a chance to model, and it would be a good place to open up feedback channels already.

"Feedback about the feedback. There were definitely times where a counselor told someone on our old team like, 'Whoa, that would spook me if you told me that after the heat of a moment.'"

Obviously, in the summer itself, scenarios could get much more dramatic and much more specific than the ones they'd run in staff training. But this had always felt useful to Maria and the rest of the Starry Sky leadership team and counselors reinforced that on their post-staff-training surveys.

"The only roleplay we've ever done is for conflict resolution," Jamie said. "I think this would be a great addition."

"People would have fun with it, pretending to be bad counselors," Laverne said. "Another opportunity for some quality relational communication." Everyone laughed, including Maria.

Samira wrote a couple more things in the communication triangle:

COMMUNICATION:
- Rational - Building rapport, trust, and positive connections with colleagues.
- Task - Sharing information, instructions, and updates to achieve specific goals.
- Growth - Providing and Receiving feedback, coaching, and learning opportunties to develop individually and collectively.

"In the interest of being able to get off of work soon," Samira said, "I'd like to move on to the fourth triangle: trust. Teams that trust each other can accomplish anything they want. They set a clear goal and they trust each other to do what's necessary to accomplish it. They're open to feedback when they're getting a little off course and, most importantly, they feel empowered to give feedback to others on the team."

"A lot of this relates back to feedback," Nico observed. "I guess it's fitting. If people were perfect, we wouldn't need any triangles."

"Very true," Samira said. "I think the four triangles each come at it from a different angle – like, trust is more about giving than receiving. If I trust you, I trust that the feedback you're giving me isn't meant to diminish, it's in the best interest of the team. But yes, they all touch on feedback." Samira said.

"Yes," Maria said. "Taking feedback is hard, but most people can summon the trust and humility for that with effort. Giving feedback, though, that's even harder. People do know what needs to be said and usually they know how to say it, too. But they're afraid that no matter how they say it, they'll be judged as some kind of brutal jerk. That's a no-trust environment. And we can't have that," Maria said.

Stu's eyes left the paper and Maria turned to follow his gaze. Their waiter was approaching again with a full platter of food. Maria slid her notebook out of the way as a heaping plate of glistening steak, fresh vegetables, and sumptuous mashed potatoes was set in front of her.

Samira was looking hungrily at her own dish. "I won't say terribly much more on trust, but there's a bit more to discuss. Feel free to dive in while I write some stuff down, though."

There was a moment of hesitation before Laverne shrugged and sliced into her steak, followed by Nico, Jamie, and Maria taking their first bites of their food. Maria's steak was flavorful and cooked just right. Stu was the only one who waited to eat.

"Go ahead, Stu," Samira prodded.

"If your food gets cold, so does mine," he replied.

"That's very gallant and very unnecessary," Samira said. "Go ahead and eat, there are just a couple more things." Stu acquiesced and cut into his salmon. Samira's dish was sizzling on her plate.

"You should eat too, though," Maria said.

"I'm good, I'll eat in a few," Samira replied.

"No, like you really should eat," Maria repeated. "This is a team dinner, not dinner and a show."

The other faces around the table were smiling lightly. They might have let the show play out, so to speak, but it seemed like they agreed with Maria that it was a little uncomfortable sitting there with gourmet meals ready to be eaten, while Samira worked away at the triangles. Samira tried a bite of her food. Her face relaxed, as if the food had broken her out of a triangle-laden trance. They passed a few minutes in casual conversation before everyone's eyes started wandering back to the unfinished diagram.

Samira seemed to take that as her signal to unpack the final bullet point in the trust section. She explained that the relational aspect of trust was most important, but trust was also about the theoretically simple, yet confoundingly elusive act of doing what one said one was going to do. Taking on tasks and then failing to accomplish them was a severe obstruction of trust. So, while Maria was the head of the leadership team, and the leadership team had various supervisory roles throughout camp, a trusting organization didn't need its leaders to constantly breathe down the necks of their employees to make sure responsibilities were being fulfilled.

"Triangles are looking good," Maria said.

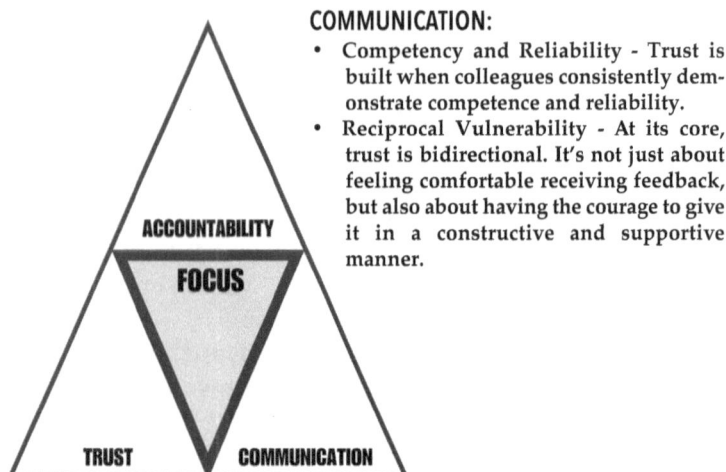

COMMUNICATION:
- Competency and Reliability - Trust is built when colleagues consistently demonstrate competence and reliability.
- Reciprocal Vulnerability - At its core, trust is bidirectional. It's not just about feeling comfortable receiving feedback, but also about having the courage to give it in a constructive and supportive manner.

"It's not quite over," Samira said. "The cool thing about the way I've drawn it out, if I do say so myself, is that the triangles can be moved around. The four parts of this model can take on different levels of importance at different times. The one that a team is working on the most is in the center."

"Are we going to have this up in the meeting room? Actual triangles that we're moving around?" Nico asked, inquisitively.

"Could be a good idea, if you all are liking this framework," Maria said. "I like it myself. Like, maybe we already have pretty good communication as a team. That's definitely been my experience so far. But what else can we focus on this summer?"

"I think you just said it," Stu added. "Focus. We have this new unified goal. Growth of the whole person. I think if everyone is keyed in on that, the other triangles—or, not triangles, tenets—will come more easily; but not vice versa."

"I hear that," Maria said. "Does anyone have another opinion?"

Jamie was chewing, and Maria looked at him without necessarily meaning to, causing him to chew rapidly and swallow in an effort to contribute. "Maybe accountability," he said, clearing his throat. "Like with what we agreed on regarding activity instruction. If activity leaders aren't holding to that, then it's an issue, but I'm not opposed to focus. I think our broader goal is most important."

Samira and Nico were nodding. Laverne said, "Hear, hear."

"I think you're right on both things, Jamie," Maria said. "Accountability is always important, and it's on us to take the actions we discussed every day. But I personally think focus is what we most need this summer."

"As y'all said, they interplay," Laverne said, shrugging. "I'm not gonna die on any hill for which one we draw in the center."

"I don't think anybody's dying on any hills," Maria said. "I'd still love to hear your opinion, though."

Laverne smirked. "Focus, then. Samira already drew it in the center anyway."

Maria looked at the paper again. Samira had indeed set up the other three triangles around the focus one by default. "Did you do that on purpose?" Maria asked, grinning.

"Maybe," Samira replied.

"Well, I agree anyway," Maria said. "It's a transition era. We need to be totally focused on our new intentions."

"All right, so focus in the middle?" Samira asked. Nobody objected. She wrapped up her diagram with a final sweep of her pen:

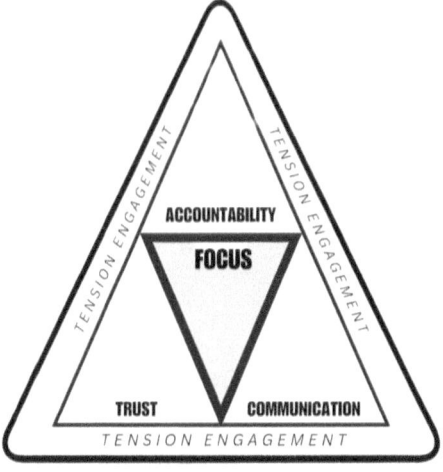

"One last thing; all the triangles support effective engagement in tension, as Maria says, which allows us to build trust, stay accountable to each other, communicate well, and keep focused on a shared goal," Samira explained. "When we engage with tension, the model stays together. But if we don't have the hard conversations with each other, then the big triangle weakens." She dipped her pen back to the paper, almost slashing through the larger triangle before apparently deciding not to ruin her drawing for the sake of a point.

"The model only works if we commit to the full version—all four triangles and the tension engagement—otherwise we'll see conflict and division." Samira then carefully slid the paper into her backpack and smiled reassuringly at the team.

"How does everyone feel?" Maria asked. "Better than after the panel, at least?"

There were nods and a few chuckles.

"I'm ready to get triangular," Laverne said.

"This really helped, Samira," Stu added, more helpfully. "Thank you for sharing. I'm glad you stuck with it."

"Okay then," Maria said, grinning. She raised her glass of water. "Enough shop talk. Let's enjoy dinner. To Blue Trail!"

"To Blue Trail!" the team echoed.

CHAPTER 8

A SHIFT IN THE ROOM

MARIA was about to tell herself that it felt "real" now, but she'd thought that at least ten times since she started the process of assuming the directorship of Blue Trail. It felt real when she first visited the camp. It felt much more real when she signed the loan from the bank. It felt even more real when she logged on to the first online meeting with the leadership team. And when they all learned so much together at the ACA conference.

But nothing to this point quite matched the feeling she had right now, staring from the directors' table in Blue Trail's dining hall outward onto the gaggle of staff that loosely populated the rest of the long tables. The din wasn't quite as loud as it would be when the campers arrived, but Maria was pleased to see that over the course of their first breakfast, the volume in the room had increased as the veteran counselors—who were already chatting it up with their friends and familiar faces—welcomed newer staff into their conversation.

"Five more minutes?" Jamie asked.

"Yeah, five," Maria confirmed.

Jamie raised his hands to his mouth and shouted "FIVE MINUTES!" The rest of the leadership team echoed, as did a few counselors. Maria was pleased to see how quickly everyone started bussing their own tables, running their silverware up to the trays at the kitchen counter, piling up their cups in a neat stack, and once the surface had been cleared of dishes, sliding a wet rag down the table, hand to hand. This was something they did at Starry Sky, too, a thrice-daily ritual of teamwork and care for their spaces.

She'd already officially introduced herself last night over dinner. The reception had been tentative but warm. It occurred to her that, unlike in a usual summer, everyone on staff was unfamiliar with her. Even those with experience were starting fresh, somewhat.

A few senior counselors, also known as SCs, had come up after dinner to welcome her more informally. One of them, Miguel, seemed to be the star of Camp Blue Trail. He was 21, promoted to unit head of the youngest cohort of cabins before last summer. His name had been dropped in several meetings with the leadership team, and he was always spoken of glowingly. He had hugged Nico the moment they saw each other and Maria immediately read that they were perhaps the tightest friends out of anyone on staff. In her own conversation with Miguel, he had come off as warm, charming, and ready to contribute to whatever Maria wished to do this summer. He seemed like a true team player. And he was truly charismatic, the kind of counselor whose influence of their peers was perhaps greater than, or at least different than, a first-summer director could achieve.

Maria knew he would be an invaluable member of their staff this year and made it a point to ask him questions about his life outside of camp, as well. He was in college in California, but not at the same school as Nico. He planned to study early childhood education in grad school starting next year and he had two younger sisters on staff at neighboring camps (Why not Blue Trail? she had wondered). Maria needed to forge a human connection with every counselor, but especially with a clear leader such as Miguel.

Currently, he was laughing at a joke that one of the CITs at his table had told. Maria hadn't heard the joke, but she saw the impact a simple laugh had on the counselor-in-training's body language. He sat up straighter, yet the tension in his body released. He was smiling lightly. People wanted to make Miguel laugh and he was clearly the kind of person for whom laughter came quite easily.

Maria and Samira had gotten to the dining hall before anyone else and posted the day's schedule, which they'd also laid out verbally the night before. Their values around focus and communication—clarity—extended to something as simple as a daily schedule. Everyone needed to know exactly what was supposed to be happening when, and a posted schedule also helped people who were forgetful or, more importantly, anxious.

The first item on their agenda was non-confrontational language, which would be led by Maria and Samira. Maria would welcome contributions from the rest of the leadership team, as well as the experienced counselors. At Starry Sky, the veterans on staff would often jump in with a raised hand, offering anecdotes or additions to whatever was being said, and Maria, Robyn, and Lane were always grateful. It meant the counselors were engaged, and it made them feel like leaders, which, of course, they were.

Five minutes had expired. Maria grabbed a microphone from its hook on a pillar by the directors' table and called for everyone to start heading out to the picnic area. It was a mild, sunny morning and there was no reason they couldn't do everything they needed to do today outside. Much to her relief, everyone seemed to hear her on her first try through the microphone, and the staff drifted outside and sat down, clump by clump, on the benches and tables that dotted the partially-shaded picnic area.

Before they started the non-confrontational language crash course, Maria ceded the floor to Jamie, who enthusiastically led a few quick name games. By the end of their third game—a staff-wide rock-paper-scissors battle royale—the mood was noticeably more spirited and happy. Jamie called for everyone to sit next to someone they didn't know or hadn't talked to yet, then gave way for Maria and Samira to speak once again.

"Hey everyone," Maria said. "I'm so excited for this week and so glad that you are all here. As a leadership team, we're always really pumped about staff training, just to spend a week getting to know all of you and really coming together, all of us, as the leaders of this camp. As you all know, it's my first summer here at Blue Trail, and I know that many of you have stacked up a lot of years here."

Maria noticed Miguel and several others smiling. Although she knew the staff as a whole didn't carry a lot of Blue Trail experience, at the very least, it seemed like there were some veterans among the senior counselors.

"As much as we," Maria continued, motioning to the rest of the leadership team, "hope to share with you, I know that you all will share so many wonderful things with me about how Blue Trail runs, and I'm looking forward to learning from all of you. I know we're going to have a really great summer. I know we're going to create a place that makes everyone—campers and staff alike—feel special, loved, like they can grow, and could spend summer after summer here.

With that said, I'll pass the metaphorical mic to Samira, who's going to lead us into our first topic of discussion today."

Several people looked like they didn't know whether they should applaud. A few of them did start to clap, then stopped quickly once they realized it didn't seem to be the right move. Maria realized it must have been a bit strange for these counselors, as young as 16, to hear her say things like "I want to build trust." But Maria had the experience to know that announcing your intention to build trust and following through on the actions you say you're going to do to accomplish that, was exactly how one builds trust quickly.

"Thank you," Samira said graciously when Maria stepped a bit to the side. "Hey, everyone. Once again, I'm Samira, I'm the new social worker. During the offseason I'm a high school counselor and I'm thrilled to have the opportunity to be part of this beautiful place during the summers. Like Maria, I'm joining Blue Trail from Camp Starry Sky in Colorado and I've heard so much already from the other leaders here about how incredibly talented the staff is here, year after year." Her voice was light and genuine. A few CITs and counselors nearest to her were smiling and attentive. She hadn't said anything truly inspiring, but it was easy to feel at ease when Samira was talking.

"So, as a social worker and as a school counselor," she said, "I deal a lot with emotions, and you camp counselors know more than anyone that just because it's summer vacation doesn't mean that camp is stress-free, right?" A wry laugh rippled through the crowd. "No, most definitely not stress-free. Campers get amped up, we get amped up with each other, you all might get amped up about us ... there's tension. We could say that our goal is to go a summer without anyone feeling sad, mad, homesick, or frustrated with a friend, but that's just not realistic. We're all human beings, with human flaws and human emotions, and all of us contribute to the energy of camp. So, yes, there will be tension. The question that keeps a social worker up at night is, how do we engage with that tension in a way that makes everyone involved feel validated, safe, and like they're creating a solution, rather than being shut down or getting into a conflict?"

Maria took note of the natural way Samira had created a distinction between tension and conflict. She was glad that her theory on the difference had stuck and after hearing what Samira said, how she'd posed "conflict" as a bad possibility, she too felt fearful of the word.

"How many people have heard the phrase 'non-confrontational language' before?" Samira asked.

A good chunk of hands went up. Well under half the staff, but enough to surprise Maria. She was especially pleased to see quite a few younger counselors raising their hands. Samira looked at her, silently inviting her to jump back in.

"Would anyone like to share what that phrase means to them?" Maria asked. "Yeah, Lucy."

Lucy, a gangly first-year CIT who had come in second in the rock-paper-scissors game, lowered her hand. "Isn't it basically, like, talking in a way that makes people feel like you're not coming at them?"

"Yeah, that's pretty much it," Maria said. "It's kind of in the definition, right? Confrontation. Conflict. We're trying to avoid true conflict as much as possible. We're going to disagree on things, sure. We're going to have tension. Campers are going to get mad at us and each other, but we want to give you all the tools to address tension effectively, without it boiling over into any thorny conflicts. Let me ask you this: Does anyone have an example of some interpersonal tension from their experience, either at camp or somewhere else?"

There was a long pause. Maria felt a brief twinge of regret; was she asking people to dig up old tiffs too soon? But then Miguel's hand slowly came up.

"Miguel, go ahead," Maria said invitingly.

"Yeah, um, I'll just give a super common scenario. A couple years ago I had a co-counselor in my cabin group who was having a little trouble connecting to the kids," Miguel said. "And this person was pretty open about it and leaned on us for help, but some other counselors were making fun of him behind his back. And he found out. So, then it got even harder because he felt so much pressure every time he talked to a kid, you know, he felt like everyone was watching and observing. It really wasn't good."

"Thank you so much for sharing that," Maria said. Gossip among counselors was indeed a very common, and very damaging, scenario. "How did you engage with the tension?" she asked.

"Well, first I pulled the one counselor aside and just told him, like, keep going, I know you love being here and I want to help you find ways to feel more comfortable. And then, well, I talked with the others who were making fun of him and told them it wasn't cool."

"And, would you be willing to share how you talked to them? I know you're bravely in the spotlight here, but I think this is such a strong example to unpack."

"Um, it was definitely not non-confrontationally," he said sheepishly. There was a staff-wide laugh. Jamie and Laverne were shaking their heads, but chuckling. Maria grinned, but then noticed that Nico had grimaced and put his forehead in his fingers.

"Okay, so maybe we don't need to hear exactly what was said," Maria said.

"No, probably not."

"But how'd it go?"

"For the one counselor, things started looking up. By the end of the summer he was probably the kids' favorite in our cabin. But the ones who I called out didn't come back the following summer."

Miguel seemed to feel badly; Maria wanted to tell him she was sure there were other reasons for those counselors not returning, but she didn't want to drag this into personal territory in front of everyone. Still, the story spoke to something central. Blue Trail had many people on staff who were supportive of others and enthusiastic about their jobs. But, by and large, people didn't quite have the trust or communication skills needed for everyone to feel comfortable going through the waves of growth that were inevitable over a multi-year camping career.

"I'm grateful for that reflection," Samira said. "It's a tough thing, figuring out what to say to our coworkers—our friends—when something's not going the way it should. Or even getting the courage to say something at all. That's why we wanted to talk about it this week. We want you all to have the tools to deal with tension without gossiping; to say something hard to someone without making them feel put down."

"Yeah, without gossip, another key point," Maria said. "It's really, really easy to fall into gossip when we're at camp. We're all in high-stress jobs and when someone is doing something that makes our job even more stressful, the human response is frustration. I get that. But gossip is going to be a nonstarter here. It destroys trust, it doesn't solve problems and it's rarely as secretive as you think."

There hadn't been that many firings during Maria's tenure at Starry Sky. But she knew Robyn and Lane had fired multiple people in the past for gossip. They felt strongly that it was a very serious offense and Maria had come to agree. But she didn't want to threaten firings, even abstractly, in the first hour of staff training.

She pivoted to a more positive framing.

"Like Samira said, we want you all to be able to go up to someone and say, to their face, 'Hey, can we chat for a second? I've noticed something I'd like to talk about.'"

Another CIT, Patrick, was raising his hand. Maria noticed a few side-eyes from one older counselor to another in the crowd.

When Maria called on him, he asked, "What about if we wanted to come talk to you about something someone else is doing? Is that gossip?"

A few people were whispering. Maria couldn't tell who, but it bothered her immensely. Not that any rational person could expect one little speech to do the trick, but she had just talked about gossip. She didn't know Patrick, but she guessed, based on the context, that he had a history of asking questions at any opportunity, even if they seemed easily answered. There was usually at least one person who fit that description at any given staff training, but it didn't annoy Maria. Those people usually turned out to be good and attentive counselors.

"That's a really good question, Patrick," she said authoritatively. She caught Samira smirking. Sometimes Maria felt like the social worker could read her mind. "Obviously, I have an open door. I want to support any of you with anything you need support on, right? But, you know in school, when a teacher says something like, 'ask three people first before you ask me for the answer?'"

Patrick was nodding vigorously.

"Well, you don't have to ask three people, but unless you see something, or something happens to you, that needs action from someone higher up in the chain of command, we want you to feel empowered with the right tools and techniques to navigate it yourself. But I'm here, Samira's here, Jamie's here, your senior counselor will be there. You can ask them to help you find the words. What we don't want is people just sharing stories that hurt others' reputation without making constructive efforts toward a solution. But no, telling one of the directors or the social worker is not gossip. If you have something that needs action from the leadership team, come right to us, but come with specifics. We can't really act on 'Someone is generally being a bad counselor.' Does that answer the question?"

"Yeah, thanks!" Patrick said.

"Anyone else have any questions before we move into a bit of practice?" Maria asked. Nobody raised their hand.

Samira went to her binder, which was lying on the bench where she'd been sitting, and slid out a stack of papers. She handed half to Maria and the two of them walked around the little crowd of counselors handing out sheets one by one.

"What we're handing you is a list of some phrases that, we think, most would consider to be non-confrontational," Samira said. "Do you have to use these exact words every time? No. But hopefully you can get the vibe of what non-confrontational language sounds like from this sheet. And if you don't, we're gonna try it out in just a bit. But we'll give you a minute to look over the sheet."

Samira had been the one to write up the table of phrases, and Maria hadn't gotten the chance to look at it before this moment, but she eagerly scanned the page now.

INSTEAD OF . . .	TRY SAYING . . .
You need to do this . . .	Perhaps we could consider . . .
Fix this! Your____work has been pretty bad lately.	Can we talk about how to improve . . .
You're not seeing this correctly. You're wrong.	From my perspective . . . I see this in a different way.
That's not going to work.	I appreciate that option, here are my concerns . . .
You make me so mad. It drives me crazy when . . .	I feel . . . I get upset when . . .
We are too far apart. We can't agree.	I feel as though____could be getting in our way.
That makes no sense.	Help me understand how that would work.

MORE SENTENCE STARTERS

- I'm really nervous/scared/uncomfortable to say this, but…

- Can we talk for a moment? I noticed something I'd like to discuss with you.

- When you said _____ , what was the purpose be hind it?

- This is what I understand you to be saying … Is that accurate?

- I just felt something shift in the room, did anyone else feel that way, too?

- I noticed that something you did/said may have been hurtful/offensive to others and wanted to discuss it with you.

- Today you made a comment using a term that many would find hard to hear. I was hoping to learn more about your intent and to share my perspective.

- It seems like some people might have had a reaction to that.

Maria thought it was as good or better of a list than she could have put together herself, but looking at the faces of the staff, she saw a lot of skepticism. A few people were smirking. Some had their brows furrowed as they read. She understood why. For people used to conflict or avoidance of tension, it was difficult to imagine walking up to a coworker and saying something along the lines of what was on the sheet.

She gave the staff another minute to examine the table before speaking again.

"Okay," Maria said. "I'm gonna borrow from our table here. I felt something shift in the room. Did anyone feel like this was super silly? Like, you can't really picture saying any of these to your friends?"

At first, nobody took the invitation. Then, with trepidation, a few of the oldest counselors raised their hands. Finally, with their eyes flitting from raised hand to raised hand, most of the counselors and CITs joined their older peers in expressing that, yes, non-confrontational language seemed a little silly.

Maria was about to address this, but Samira spoke instead. "Hey, it's okay, we're engaging with tension, right? I made this sheet. I want to hear why you think it's strange."

Another long silence passed before Ava, one of their oldest senior counselors, lifted her hand. "I wouldn't say it's strange, but I think I'm just having a little trouble seeing how this would feel natural, and not like," she looked up, as if searching for the right words in the sky. "I don't know, like someone is very clearly trying not to offend when they have something potentially offensive to say."

Miguel had his hand raised, too. He spoke without Samira or Maria calling on him. "Yeah, going off that, I think if I heard someone come up to me with that, I'd just kind of roll my eyes," he said, before quickly adding, "on the inside."

Samira spread her hands. "Great! Thank you! This is the number one criticism that's leveled at ideas like this. It's kind of fake, right? Why don't we just come right out and say what we're wanting to say?" Samira mused.

"Yeah, just come right out and say it," another head counselor, Lainey, echoed in agreement.

"Well," Maria ventured. "Are you all in the habit of just coming right out and saying it?"

Snickers rippled through the crowd. Maria pressed her advantage.

"I'm serious," she said. "If you all are really comfortable going up to each other and expressing, straight-up, what's bothering you, then we can skip this part of training. If you all can honestly tell me that Camp Blue Trail is a place where everyone just hashes out their beef right away, professionally and respectfully, we'll move on."

Nobody cheered the idea of moving on. Maria grinned knowingly. "We don't really do that, do we?" she asked. "Why do people tend to not do that, Samira?"

"Well, beyond the fact that it would truly be hurtful to express the unfiltered force of our frustration sometimes," Samira marched over to Maria and got into her face dramatically, "'Hey, Maria, you really suck at getting campers ready to move to their next activity, how 'bout some situational awareness?' People generally resist the opportunity to be completely honest with someone they're having tension with.

"Like we've said, it's hard to stand up and say that something needs to be done differently. So this sheet isn't only here to tell you what to say, but now that we've all looked at this, and we're about to practice it, we know that when we hear a coworker say something like, 'Hey, can we talk about something that happened yesterday?' it means that, yes, a difficult conversation might be about to happen. No way around it. But it also means, 'Hey, I'm coming to you with some curiosity about something you did, but it's not an attack on you,' it's all in the interest of us having a better camp and growing as counselors."

See discussion activity 8.1 at the end of the chapter

Maria checked her watch. They'd spent more time than they'd hoped going over the theory, so she quickly explained the practical portion of this lesson. They were going to split into smaller groups, each led by someone on the leadership team, and run through several scenarios so that each person in the group got the chance to be on both the giving and receiving end of some non-confrontational language exercises. The receivers were encouraged to begin the engagement with an unreceptive facade. This would be a good opportunity for the senior counselors to take the reins as leaders as well. Maria had instructed the rest of the leadership team to mine scenarios from the veterans in their groups and, as much as possible by the end of the practice session, cede the supervisory floor to them.

The groups broke off, scattering around the picnic area. Maria's group, which included Miguel, was doing pretty well implementing the non-confrontational language. There were a few laughs during the first few scenarios, but by the fourth or fifth runthrough, the novelty seemed to have expired, and with it the comedy of the situations. Any laughs that followed were genuine and good-natured. People chuckled when the person on stage, so to speak, grasped for words, but Miguel and the other experienced counselors in the group were capable with the feedback and very encouraging of the younger staff.

"Remind me your name again? I'm so sorry," Miguel said, after one CIT finished his runthrough of a scenario in which he played a senior counselor who had noticed one of their cabin coworkers exhibiting some favoritism.

"Leo," the CIT said.

"Leo, thank you. I mean," he looked at Maria, and Maria nodded, silently encouraging him to take the lead, "I think that was really good, your tone was great, the substance was great, hit the nail on the head with explaining in a nice way why it's a bad look to just hang around a few kids. I'd just say you could offer, as the senior counselor in the scenario, to just, you know, be of more assistance in helping this counselor build relationships with more kids. Because it's probably not something this counselor is doing willingly, they're just trying to do what's comfortable. But it's not quite where we want to be. So, anyways, as a senior counselor, part of the job is to make your co-counselors know that you have their back."

Leo was nodding rapidly, his face stony. Maria was about to step in and offer some encouragement, but Miguel beat her to it, clearly noticing the same thing she had.

"I'm only offering that little bit of suggestion because the rest of what you did was so good. Perfect delivery. If I were the counselor I would feel very non-confronted. Joel, did you feel confronted?"

Joel, another CIT, had taken on the role of the counselor who'd been playing favorites in the scenario, and he shook his head emphatically.

"Awesome," Miguel finished. "Yeah, you got it down, Leo, so you get a little bit of senior counselor tricks of the trade. Sorry, Maria? Did you want to add anything?"

Maria shrugged. "I think you covered it," she said proudly. Then she turned to Leo. "You definitely had the spirit of non-confrontation down, and what Miguel said doesn't just apply to senior counselors. If you're a CIT and you notice someone is struggling, one of the best ways for someone to not feel deflated after you bring up some tension with them is to offer ways for improvement. That gets people thinking about action, not just self-defeat."

Nico's group was closest to Maria's, and out of the corner of her eye she saw that the trips director still looked a little deflated himself. Come to think of it, he'd looked morose since Miguel told his story back in the large group.

"Great job, Leo," she said. Then, to Miguel, "Got another scenario? I'm gonna circle around for a minute."

"For sure," he said.

Maria arrived at Nico's group just as he was wrapping up a bit of feedback on a counselor's performance. She hadn't been there for the scenario or the rest of Nico's feedback, but what she observed was fairly sparse, like he hadn't really been listening and was pulling vague generalities out of thin air. His voice sounded not just casual, but disinterested and monotonous. She felt like a professor who'd called on a student who hadn't done the reading.

Ava, the senior counselor who'd risen to the challenge of questioning Samira's phrasing sheet, was part of Nico's group, and Maria asked if she'd take over for a minute while she spoke with Nico. Ava agreed enthusiastically and Maria and Nico walked over to, fittingly, the trips bulletin board to talk where they wouldn't be overheard.

"Are you okay?" Maria asked.

"Yeah, why?"

"Well, from my point of view, you seem a little less interested in this than you have been in anything I've done with you previously, and I'm wondering if that rings true to you. And if so, why?"

"I'm all good," he said flatly.

"Okay, well then I'm going to ask you to be a little more generous with your feedback to the counselors in this activity."

"Noted. But, come on, you saw maybe 15 seconds of me talking."

"How do you feel about the feedback you've given the rest of the session?"

He shifted. "I feel good."

"Okay. Do you mind if I sit with y'all for a bit?"

At this, Nico scowled. "That makes me feel like you don't trust me."

Samira's words from their dinner in Denver echoed in Maria's head. A trusting team allowed its members to accomplish their responsibilities without constant surveillance. If she was honest, she didn't trust that Nico was telling the truth. It wasn't just the 15 seconds worth of talking she'd heard. His body language, normally relaxed and attentive, had been more closed off and tense than she'd ever seen.

Still, she decided to give him some grace. "You're right," Maria said. "I'll keep circling. If you do want to talk, I'm here."

Nico looked to the side, pursing his lips. Maria could almost see his thoughts, see him debating whether to grit his teeth and work less effectively, or risk showing vulnerability.

"Look, I don't want to make a big deal out of this," he finally said, "but Miguel's story about that counselor who couldn't bond with the kids kind of upset me."

Maria nodded. She herself had been wondering whether it had been a mistake to ask for tough stories from past summers so soon. "Okay, yeah, I can see why it might have felt weird to ask people to dredge up old tension like that," she said.

"No, it's not that," Nico said. "That idea was fine for the exercise. It was probably valuable. But ... the counselor in the story was me."

"Oh, wow."

Nico grimaced. "Yeah. I mean, look, I don't know how much you know about how and why Director Dan made me trips director, or maybe you can guess, but I wasn't the biggest fan of the counselor life here. After my first summer as a senior counselor I was pretty sure that I wasn't going to come back for another year. The thing I loved most about camp was the trips. I never really got into a groove with the day-to-day of cabin life. Dan didn't want to lose me, so he carved out the trips director post for me. It was a win-win. I pretty much sucked as a counselor, and the camp benefited from my work last summer."

"I'm sure you didn't suck," Maria said kindly.

"Well, let's just say Miguel was pretty nice to say that I was the kids' favorite counselor by the end of that summer. I certainly didn't feel that I was."

"So Miguel's story reminded you of a time where you didn't feel comfortable at camp."

"Yeah. And ..." he was avoiding Maria's eyes again. "I'm sorry for looking disengaged. This is a good activity. The last thing I want to have is, like, a big pity party right now."

"Nico, being honest is not a pity party, and it's okay that what Miguel shared bothered you. Tell me more."

Nico sighed. "Look at him, he's senior counselor extraordinaire, and part of me feels like I failed upward."

"I understand. Miguel is Miguel. I'm glad to have him on our staff and I'm sure you are too. But," Maria looked at him intently, "You didn't fail upward. Like you said, Dan's decision was a win-win. He saw your passion for the outdoors and for the ways people grow on trips and put you in a spot to maximize that for as many people as possible. When people fail upward, they don't usually have positions created for them."

"True. Very true."

"Do you need help brainstorming what to say to Miguel?"

"I wasn't going to say anything," Nico said. "I'd look like I have the biggest ego in the world, getting offended by one anonymous story."

"I made plenty of mistakes working at camp. Even if it were anonymous, I wouldn't love it if someone just told a weird Maria story in front of everyone either."

"There's a difference between not loving it and actually, like, pulling someone aside over it. This kind of thing just isn't something we usually address."

"I hear that, but I can also see that your feelings might be affecting how you lead this activity. And also, practicing feedback in small moments is good. It all helps build trust. Maybe this isn't something that would've been addressed in the past, but I think it should be now."

Nico took another long moment to consider. "He's my best friend at camp."

"And if you had hurt your best friend, wouldn't you want to make amends?"

"Yes," Nico said, more resolutely. "So you think I should talk to him? Or are you, like, asking me to talk to him?"

Maria could sense that he'd be reluctant to confront his friend unless she ordered him to, but she wasn't keen to do that. Nico was part of the leadership team. He was young, talented, and invaluable to the camp's future. She wanted him to see the importance of initiating this conversation himself and to understand that he had the power, not only as Miguel's friend, but as his hierarchical superior, to express his discomfort at an action that Miguel had taken.

"I think that, given what we've just talked about as an entire staff, it would be a really great thing for you to do, to go up to someone who you consider a close friend and say 'Hey, I'm kind of nervous to say this, but the story you shared made me feel a little vulnerable,'" Maria said.

Nico's expression softened toward openness, rather than fear.

"You certainly don't have to pull him aside now. Or even today," Maria said gently. "I do think that internally resolving to bring this up with him would allow you to feel more present in the activity that's happening right now."

"Okay, I will," Nico said. "I'll talk to him. I'm sorry, I know I can't let things throw me like that when we're trying to train a staff."

Maria smiled at him and said, "Thank you. It's okay. As we've talked about, things are going to bother us this summer. It's just about what we do next to resolve it."

"I hear you," Nico said. "I'm going to head back to my group now, if that's cool."

"Of course."

Nico walked away, standing a little taller and moving a little faster than he had on the way over. Maria took another moment before rejoining her group. She hoped that what she knew about trust held true for Nico. He and Miguel had years of friendship to fall back on. Friends trusted each other, and trust meant that you could have hard conversations and not lose sight of the good relationship you still had.

Building a Culture of Feedback

Think: How would you describe the current state of feedback in your organization? Is it open, honest, and constructive? Or are there barriers or discomfort around giving and receiving feedback?

Analyze: Identify specific behaviors that you as a leader can demonstrate, such as actively seeking feedback, acknowledging mistakes openly, and celebrating learning opportunities.
Consider: What concrete steps can you take, individually and as a team, to foster a more open and constructive feedback culture?

Challenge: What else can you do to help your co-workers engage in active reflection, encourage collaborative action, and inspire them to become champions of a culture where feedback is a tool for growth and development, not simply a formality?

CHAPTER 9

UNDER THE UMBRELLA OF FUN

T HE next thing Maria wanted to accomplish was to bring the entire staff on board with the stated goal that she and the leadership team had agreed upon during the offseason: to help everyone who passed through Blue Trail's welcome arch grow into better, more skillful leaders and people. To do this, she'd need Stu's data from the survey that had been sent out to all the parents, of both campers and counselors, at the end of the prior few summers. Maria, Stu, and the rest of the leadership team had gone over the data and it supported their collective hypothesis: Those parents who noticed a difference in their child from when they said goodbye to when they welcomed them back home were more likely to send their child back for another summer.

Of course, part of the reason that Maria and the team had been so eager to dive into this data was to stop the unfortunate trend of campers and staff leaving Blue Trail. If they could understand why people left, they could understand why people stayed. Maria had made it clear in the very first team meeting that she didn't want the staff to know the camp was losing numbers. They probably already knew, but the last thing she wanted was for the counselors to behave like the camp was in crisis or, even worse, like they were resigned to sail on a doomed voyage.

Maria still thought it was important that when she and Stu talked about the big goal with the staff, their idea was reinforced with evidence. It was very possible to share the data without sharing the foreboding flip-side.

Stu glided into the center of the picnic area, swapping places with Samira, who took his spot on one of the benches.

"I'll reintroduce myself as well," he said. "I'm Stu, I'm the parent liaison here. It's my job to make sure all the campers' parents, and yours, know about all the fun and meaningful things that go on here every day, and to answer their questions and inform them if anything's gone awry.

"I'm also the guy who's writing the newsletter, posting pictures to our social media platforms and website, and whose lovely voice parents will hear when they call the main office phone.

"Most importantly for our next part of staff training though, it is my job to design, distribute, and analyze the surveys that all camp parents fill out after each summer, plus the ones that you and the campers do, but for this particular section of the day I want to focus on the parent surveys."

"This is a question that everyone on the leadership team answered in our very first meeting together back in February," Maria said. "I'd love to hear from some of our veterans on staff. What about Blue Trail, or camp in general, makes you come back summer after summer?"

Maria was happy to see many hands lift into the air almost immediately. It seemed like everyone on staff who had been to Blue Trail for more than one summer, whether it was as a counselor or as a camper-turned-CIT, wanted to contribute.

"Okay, let's go rapid-fire," she said. "Ava, go ahead."

"My friends."

"Yes, friends. Kelsey, what about you?"

"Yeah, friends. And the activities. If I weren't here I'd be working some boring, repetitive job. And in my free time I'd just watch TV."

"There we go," Maria chuckled. "Glad to have you here, and not stuffing grocery bags or something." The crowd laughed. "Someone else. Yeah, Patrick."

"Camp helps me get out of my comfort zone," Patrick said. Much to Maria's appreciation, nobody laughed at him this time. Hopefully his answer rang true to people. It was getting closer to what Maria and Stu would be talking about with the data.

"Nice, Patrick," Maria said. "I feel that one. I always like to say that no matter how old you are, camp gives you exactly what you need. Let's get a couple more people. Miguel!"

Miguel smiled. "Above all, camp is just fun. The people, the activities, that's why I keep coming back, I know there's no way I'm gonna have more fun anywhere else."

Many people murmured their assent. Maria was glad to see this, too. She'd been a counselor; it could be a very stressful, always-on job. Obviously there was a great deal to juggle as a member of the leadership team and especially as a director, but it was good to know that so many people on staff felt that, above all, Blue Trail was a fun, joyous place. As she knew from the data, however, fun alone wasn't enough to keep people coming back.

She couldn't sleep on the importance of fun, though. "Yes, that's a good one. I don't think anyone would keep coming back if they weren't having any fun. One more person, and then we're going to bring in some data."

Mychele, a counselor, raised her hand. "Kind of what Patrick said. And what you said. I learn things about myself that I didn't know before each summer."

"Yes. Absolutely. What are some of those things, if you feel like sharing?" Maria asked.

Mychele leaned forward, resting her elbows on her thighs. "Well, I learned that I can be good with kids. I didn't know how I'd do as a counselor, to be honest, but I wanted to try, and I feel like I made good connections last summer. I was never a camper here, I'd never spent more than a couple days away from my parents before last summer, so I learned how to rely on myself and my friends more, yeah."

"That's beautiful, Mychele," Maria said. "That's exactly what we want everyone to be feeling about themselves when they leave camp. That they're capable of learning and doing things that they didn't know they could. Okay, we're going to give you all another sheet of paper now."

She and Stu sent two stacks of paper around the loose circle of counselors. When the extras had been returned to Maria, she set them aside and nodded quickly at Stu, who stepped forward more.

"What you see on the paper you're holding is actual data that I've compiled from the last three summers of parent surveys," Stu explained. "Parents of campers and parents of counselors don't get the exact same survey, but there's a lot of overlap. These are the questions that appear across both."

On a scale of 1 to 5 (1 being strongly disagree, 3 being neutral, 5 being strongly agree), please rate the following statements:

My child was physically safe and secure.	4.8
My child was emotionally safe and secure.	4.2
My child had a lot of fun.	4.7
My child had meaningful relationships with peers	4.2
My child created meaningful relationships with adults.	4.3
My child grew in a noticeable way over summer (e.g., emotional intelligence, leadership and teamwork skills, activity related skills).	4.0

Stu had omitted the most concerning data point: Parents, on average, had rated the statement, "My child plans to return to Blue Trail next summer," only a 3.8. A camp could not survive if most parents were giving a hard maybe to the prospect of a return summer.

"These aren't all the questions we ask, but these are the six I consider to be the most significant," Stu said. "The ones that most align with what camps generally do and what our mission is, more specifically. As you can see, parents think we do a lot of things really well.

"On a most basic level, we keep people physically safe. We don't create an environment that's dangerous, but when accidents inevitably happen, we do a pretty good job responding and keeping parents in the loop. We'll talk more about how we do that specifically later in the week. There are a couple of changes we'd like to implement this year that are going to help us be even more communicative with parents when we—or, when I—have to tell them about any hard situations.

"Ava, Kelsey, Miguel, you all mentioned fun in some form as something that keeps you coming back every summer. Whether that's because of activities, the opportunities to make friends, or just the general camp vibe, parents seem to agree that Blue Trail is, scientifically speaking, a fun place," Stu said grandly.

As far as Maria knew, Stu didn't have any mathematics in his professional or educational background, but he really seemed to enjoy diving into this data and presenting it in such an official manner. It was like he was defending a research paper, only instead of a panel of professors and peers, it was a crowd of mostly teenagers interpreting his work. She picked up where he left off.

"The data shows that there's room for improvement as well. When we talk about safety at camp, we're also talking about emotional safety. Do campers know what to expect on a day-to-day basis? Do they trust the people around them? Do they feel supported and loved for who they are? Are their feelings validated? I look at the difference between the parents' rating for physical safety and their rating for emotional safety and I take note. This is hundreds of parents we're talking about. A 4.7 versus a 4.2 is significant.

"Same thing for the two questions on meaningful relationships; 4.2 for peers and 4.3 for adults. These are good scores; the vast majority of people are agreeing with both statements. But not a lot of strong agreement, especially compared to the statement on fun. We want those to go hand-in-hand. We want part of the fun to be creating those meaningful relationships, doing fun activities with people you love and people you're just getting to know. There's a drop-off there, which tells us that some parents are getting the impression that their kids just kind of had … "

"Superficial fun?" Laverne chimed in from the bench where the leadership team had perched.

Maria winced. She didn't want the returning counselors on staff to think that the fun they'd created was "superficial," but Laverne wasn't wrong.

"Well, I don't think fun is superficial," Maria said. "If you look under the umbrella of 'fun,' you find the opportunity to develop social skills, emotional intelligence, and problem-solving and teamwork skills, not to mention friendships and memories. 'Fun' itself isn't the main priority of a meaningful and successful camp. We need to focus on those things under the umbrella instead. That's what allows for fun to happen."

She quickly scanned the body language of the crowd. The merry mood that the non-confrontational language crash course had conjured was gone. A few people on the bench closest to her were staring at the ground. She supposed that talking so clinically about fun wasn't really many people's idea of fun.

"We're not trying to be downers," Stu said. "This data shows that we're in a good place for this summer." Maria supposed this was true, if you looked at it from a certain way. Blue Trail had proven itself to be a fun place to hang out for a summer in the woods. It needed to deepen culturally to reach essential meaning in the minds of parents and campers. And, as Robyn had said months ago, there was no such thing as a culture "tweak," but they could certainly be in a worse position. Maria liked the staff so far and was confident they'd take to the message the leadership team would be teaching throughout this week.

"At the same time, we think it's valuable to show you all this data so we can agree, as a group, on what truly keeps people coming back summer after summer," Stu continued. "Because, ultimately, we want to have everyone who sets foot on our grounds to love this place enough to make it a consistent part of their young lives."

"And the cool part is, as staff, we are the main drivers of creating that kind of place," Maria said. "So let's look at the next section on the page here, and that will further inform the mindset that all of us need to be carrying into this summer."

The next section on the page was where Stu had really dug deep into the data and tracked the correlation between parents' scores for likelihood of return and their scores for each of the six categories they'd already touched on.

Correlation of "likelihood to return" with other variables

	Physical safety	Emotional Safety	Fun	Relation-ships with Peers	Relation-ships with adults	Growth
Likelihood of return	Weak	Strong	Weak	Moderate	Strong	Strong

"I don't know if we have any people who have taken stats classes, but I can provide more precise numbers for anyone who's interested later," Stu said. "In the meantime, does anything about this table surprise anyone?"

Miguel raised his hand, grinning sheepishly. "I mean, yeah, I wouldn't expect fun to mean basically nothing."

"Not nothing, but not strongly correlated with the likelihood to return," Maria said. "As we saw, most people had a lot of fun, but that doesn't mean that everyone wants to come back."

Patrick had his hand raised. "What percentage of people come back after each summer?"

"I don't have the number off the top of my head," Maria said. She and the leadership team had, of course, discussed the number ad nauseam in recent months. "But no camp has perfect retention, and we don't really want perfect retention. Some turnover is good. We want to be bringing in new people, too. Even though all camps need retention, and, like Stu said, it is important, the goal for us to focus on is individual and collective growth. As we see here, when parents feel like their children are growing, the result is that they sign up for more summers."

Patrick's expression indicated that he'd accepted her answer as good enough.

"Growth is number one," Ava pointed out helpfully.

"Yes it is," Stu said. "In fact, all but one parent who scored the growth category at a 5 indicated that their camper would return for another summer."

"You will see, as we go through this week, that we as a leadership team have put a lot of thought into how we can create an environment that encourages growth this summer," Maria said. "From activities, to feedback, to conflict resolution, we've thought about everything that happens here from that mindset, because the evidence is kind of overwhelming."

"There are other key insights in the data as well," Stu said. "As you said, Ava, growth is what most closely correlates with likelihood of return. But, for instance, although emotional safety had only the third-highest correlation with likelihood to return, it had a very high correlation with 'meaningful relationships with adults.' Why do we think that is?"

Nobody volunteered to speak for several seconds, so Maria added, "In this case, 'adults' also refers to you, the counselors. Campers think of you as the adults at camp."

A counselor, Nora, finally sat forward and spoke. "Well, there would be lots of times where I'd try to get a kid to try a new activity and that was always easier to do when I had a really good relationship with them. The kids I was closest to listened to me, the kids that I'd just kind of chirp at when they passed by the station I was at for signups didn't listen."

"Exactly, Nora," Maria said. "The kids you were closest with trusted you. They had a meaningful relationship with you, an adult in their eyes. They felt emotionally safe to try something new at your encouragement. And what happens when we try something new?"

A few people nervously mumbled something that sounded like "growth" or "we grow." Maria took it as a win. She knew from personal experience as a college student not very many years ago that it felt weird o call out an answer, even when it was a fairly obvious question and the professor was specifically asking for it.

Miguel looked like he was sitting on a question. "I'm a little curious why you think fun seems so low on parents' priorities here," he asked.

Maria had her answer, but she wanted to give space for someone else on the leadership team to speak up, so she asked if any of them had a hypothesis.

Laverne was the one to give an answer.

"Well, before I was activities director here, I was the mom of three campers. I don't really recall what the surveys were like back then, I don't even remember that we had any, but now it's all online and easy and I would've said the same thing that the consensus seems to be saying here. Growth is most important. Did I want and need my kids to have fun during the summer? Absolutely, but that wasn't enough for me to see a place as valuable. It just wasn't my highest priority. Because they could have had fun hanging out with their neighborhood friends, playing video games in the basement. They could have had fun at a day camp at the local rec center. They could have had fun at any number of places that were closer and much cheaper than Blue Trail. But I wanted them to get some independence! Sending them off to Blue Trail, I thought, was the best way to do that. And I think I was right. The growth piece, the character building—going to a new place and having to connect with new people and try new things—that's the part that's unique to a summer camp, so Maria and Stu are right. That's what we all need to lock in on this year."

The counselors were rapt with attention. Throughout staff training so far, there had always been a slight rustling of side conversations popping up in clumps too brief and small for Maria to have the ability or desire to call back to attention. But as Laverne went on, there was not a sound from the crowd. As much as, on paper, Laverne seemed to be the least exuberant of anyone on the leadership team, Maria knew she probably carried the most respect out of any of them. When she chose to step up and talk about leadership, even in her own, slightly brusque manner, people listened. Maria hoped that she'd take the initiative to speak up more throughout the rest of the week. She'd make sure to offer ample opportunity.

"Thanks, Laverne," was all Maria felt the need to say. There was nothing more to add to what Laverne had shared. "Hold on to your sheets, everyone. Use it as a reminder. Any more questions?"

Nobody, not even Patrick, raised a hand.

CHAPTER 10

THE BIG AND DIFFICULT CONCEPT OF FEEDBACK

O VER the next two days of staff training, Maria made it her mission to have meaningful, one-on-one conversations with as many counselors as possible before their talent show on Wednesday. Tuesday had proven good for that. A great portion of the day had been spent in people's activity groups, so Maria had bounced around to the various stations—the lake, the climbing wall, the athletic fields, the arts and crafts studio—to chat it up with the counselors while they got oriented to their activities.

Maria had asked Laverne to explain, in her own words, the concept of knowledge, skills, and dispositions that Maria had laid out in their second meeting as a leadership team. If Laverne still held any resentment over the discussion they'd had about staffing, it didn't show. She seemed fully behind the idea that anyone, even someone who wasn't a future professional in the activity they were supposed to be leading, could be a competent and meaningful leader of that activity. And it seemed like the staff bought in immediately. Just before everyone split off to do mini-orientations at each of their activity stations, Maria had given the activity groups time to meet up and sketch out their first week of camp around the idea of measuring growth and teaching more technique. Each activity leader was given a printed-out schedule to complete with their plans for the week and then show it to Maria or Laverne. Maria was pleased to see that every draft schedule was packed with activities. She'd been worried that many of the activity leaders would fill the blank blocks of time with a scrawled "scrimmage" or "TBD."

Most of the staff were eager to get a little one-on-one time with the new director. Her first stop was down at the boat dock and she was pleased to see that Jacob, the head of waterskiing, was stressing the importance of safety from the get-go. This was his second summer as waterski director and she knew it would be critical to have a good working relationship with him. Waterskiing was their most popular and most high-risk activity. When she got a moment alone with him, she'd tried to learn some non-camp-related things about Jacob; it seemed as though he truly lived and breathed water skiing. He was an avid skier in the off-season, as well, having formed a waterski club at his college and placed highly as an individual in several recent tournaments. He held the Blue Trail record on the slalom course and was, as he not-so-humbly shared with her, the only person in camp capable of barefooting: skiing without skis.

Miguel would be heading up his usual post of rock climbing, and, whether he'd come up with them on the spot or not, he replied with several ideas when Maria asked him if he had any thoughts on how he could incorporate growth tracking into his activity.

"It's sort of built in," he said. "How high can you get up the wall? Can you get all the way up? Can you get up the most advanced routes? How fast? I can track all of that.

Maybe even give people little prizes. I guess that's why I love to teach climbing but hadn't realized it. There's nothing really to do in rock climbing other than grow stronger, climb higher."

See discussion activity 10.1 at the end of the chapter

Maria and Laverne both had high hopes for their newest activity, Ultimate Frisbee, which had only started up two summers prior. During those last two summers, Blue Trail hadn't had anyone on staff who played Ultimate Frisbee or disc golf in their spare time. This year, however, they had a new senior counselor, Demi, who played in college and promised to run some simple, relaxed warmup drills before they played a game. She appeared to be keenly aware of the balance she needed to strike to both allow kids to get out and play and to foster development of real skills. She'd unknowingly repeated something Laverne had said during the leadership team's meeting on activity instruction: Just launching into a game only serves those who are already practiced in the physical skills needed to succeed. Those who didn't come in with those skills would be ignored and therefore never have the chance to grow or have fun.

After she'd completed her circuit of the activity leaders and senior counselors, at mealtimes Maria took turns sitting at different tables, inserting herself within the various clumps of CITs and counselors and talking mostly about anything other than camp. She thought back to when Samira had explained the not-so-revolutionary concept of relational communication to the leadership team, how the team had asked Maria if she'd arranged that dinner in Denver simply as a means to check that box. She supposed that she had, and likewise, she was very strategically attempting to break the ice with as many counselors as possible before campers arrived. However, that didn't mean the conversations she was having weren't genuine, or that she didn't enjoy hearing about Patrick's two pet guinea pigs, or Lucy's hometown of 200 people in North Dakota, or Joel's collection of action figures that he claimed held a five-figure value, or Nora's obsession with Disney musicals, an interest Maria shared.

It reminded Maria, as staff training often did, of how simultaneously mature and very, very young the staff was. At camp, they would be entrusted with the physical and emotional safety of hundreds of children, while many were not yet adults themselves. When they finally got back home for the summer, they'd probably be scrambling to finish the summer reading that they'd had neither the energy nor desire to touch while they were at camp.

Maria noticed that the other members of the leadership team, but most notably Samira and Jamie, were doing the same, mingling with many different groups, laughing easily, mostly listening and asking questions. For Jamie, this was to be expected. Maria knew that he was charismatic and the experienced staff adored him. For him, it was likely just as much about convening with old friends and new as it was about doing due diligence and getting to know the staff. As for Samira, it was a good step toward becoming a more front-facing social worker and leader than she was at Starry Sky. She was never unfriendly, in fact, just the opposite. But there was a time when Samira would have been content to eat her staff training meals at the directors' table, where Nico, Laverne and Stu were camped out right now. Maria was pleased to see Samira taking initiative to create the reputation she desired. She expected nothing less.

Nico's engagement had returned to its normal high level after Maria's discussion with him. And after dinner on Tuesday night, Maria saw Nico having what looked like a very calm and understanding talk with Miguel by the office. The talk concluded with a handshake and a hug.

"He totally understood. It was no big deal. I just don't think he knew how insecure I was about that summer," Nico told Maria when she looped back to confirm how everything had gone.

It was the same philosophy of conflict resolution, or tension engagement, that she'd been trained on at Starry Sky as a counselor, and that she and Samira had trained the Blue

Trail staff on earlier that day. Encourage people, whether they are campers or counselors, or even leadership team members, to have their own difficult discussions, but make sure to follow up afterward. That way, you avoid the appearance of being hands-off and disinterested.

"Are you glad you talked to him?" Maria asked. When Nico smirked, Maria added, "I'm not asking that so you can pat my back about encouraging you to do so. I'm curious how you feel."

"Well, yeah, it was a good thing to do," Nico admitted. "No reason to hold a grudge going into summer. Most people are pretty reasonable when you talk to them one-on-one."

Finally, in the middle of the morning on Wednesday, Jamie took center stage as the emcee of the first annual Blue Trail Staff Training Talent Show, which the counselors had started referring to as the B.T.S.T.T.S. Personally, Maria was hoping a different acronym that had been percolating in her head—T.E.G., for tension-engage and grow—would catch on, but so far, she hadn't actually used it. In her mind, though, it could function as a sort of winking version of Samira's sentence starters. Instead of, "I noticed something earlier and I wanted to get your perspective," one could simply say, "Let's teg." For now, the much more cumbersome B.T.S.T.T.S. was all the rage. The mood was merry in the picnic area as each counselor, or group of counselors, held the floor for three minutes or less to display talents that ranged from genuine, a ballet routine from Mychele, soccer tricks from a counselor named Rosa; to the absurd, Miguel pulling out his phone, searching for a guided meditation, and reading the script completely deadpan, to the absolute hysteria of the rest of the staff, Nico included.

There was no winner of the talent show, although Maria had overheard Miguel telling a few first-year CITs that there was a $250 cash prize.

Maria left the morning feeling impressed at both the actual talents of the people on staff, who clearly led rich, passionate lives outside of camp, and the way in which every act had been applauded, every performer given numerous high fives. Halfway through the show, Maria leaned over to both Laverne (who had first proposed a staff talent show) and Nico (who had said they should hold it during staff training) and thanked them both for birthing the idea.

Thursday was the day Maria and the team had circled for a big session on the importance of feedback. At Starry Sky, Robyn and Lane had always led this part of staff training. Maria had only joined them once, in her final year there. So, Maria's natural inclination was to team up with Jamie, but, before staff training, Samira had asked her for the opportunity to be a part of leading the session. Maria had agreed, at first. This was Samira's wheelhouse, and Maria was keen on keeping her word that Samira would be given more opportunities to lead this summer. Jamie had already led much of the more administrative talks with the staff, such as emergency protocols, the layout of camp, the specific responsibilities of each level of counselor. Plus, with the talent show, he'd had plenty of chances to show all sides of his leadership style, both the charismatic and the cerebral.

Then Maria realized that she had so much trust in Samira's knowledge and passion for this particular subject that it might be good to have her lead the session by herself. After all, it was Samira who would be mostly responsible for continuing the counselors' training on emotional intelligence and leadership during the summer. She had asked to take on more of a supervisory role. Maria thought it would be smart to sit back for this one and let Samira be the main face of feedback knowledge at Blue Trail.

They had just eaten lunch. It was Taco Thursday, one of the many idiosyncratic Blue Trail traditions Maria had already come to love. This was Maria's favorite meal so far and while she had never felt the urge to say anything so lofty as "my compliments to the chef" at an actual restaurant, here she actually could give her compliments to the head chef, Miller, and she did. Samira now stood on her own at the center of the picnic area.

"One of the things that you realize when you work in camps for a long enough time," Samira began, "is that camps are probably more important for you than for the campers. We've talked a lot this week about growth. Everyone who comes through our arch, whether they're a camper or a counselor, is going to grow as a leader and as a person. I think what Laverne said a few days ago is important. We could all have fun at home, watching TV or getting a bite to eat with our friends. What camp provides is an opportunity to change for the better. And all of you, as teenagers and young adults, are at such a crucial stage in your life. At the risk of sounding dramatic, I really do see the magnitude of this every summer at camp and every day at my off-season job. This is such an important time and the growth that you all will experience this summer is much fuller, much richer, and it can be much more intentional than what the campers will experience. Camp is a fun summer getaway for everyone and like Maria said, that's really important; but, really, camps are full-on leadership academies for the staff."

A few of the older counselors were nodding. Maria had heard this sentiment expressed from parents of counselors before and hopefully the counselors had realized this little secret about camps before this moment. Maria had always believed that camp gave you exactly what you needed, no matter what age you were. But the distinction was that, when you got to be the age of a counselor, you really started to know what you needed from camp. Everyone on this staff, including herself, possessed strengths and weaknesses. Most were conscious of both. And Maria loved the way Samira had phrased it; the experience, both in camp and in life, that these counselors had already attained, would allow them to be intentional about the ways in which they grew.

"There will always be ways for each one of us to be better leaders than we already are. CITs, counselors, senior counselors, even us on the leadership team, we are all still growing and learning," Samira continued. "How many of you, while working at Blue Trail or even as a camper, have ever sat down for any kind of feedback session with an authority figure?"

Everyone in the crowd raised their hands.

"Good, good," Samira said. "As a camper, this can mean a moment when you were pulled aside by a counselor, or when a counselor highlighted your growth. And as a CIT, counselor, or SC, this would be when one of your supervisors had a sit-down with you and discussed your progress: strengths, areas of growth, how you're feeling in the cabin and at your activities. Sounds like we're all familiar with this already, which I'm really glad about. Now, my next question: Keep your hand raised if, in any of these sessions, the feedback has been something along the lines of 'great work, no notes, keep doing what you're doing.'"

Everyone's hand was still aloft. People's eyes were roving about, meeting and darting away like bees jumping from flower to flower. It didn't seem like anyone knew what Samira would say next; the counselors' expressions were those of someone who didn't know whether they were about to be in trouble.

Samira was beaming. "Okay. Very nice. You can all lower your hands now. This means a couple things. One, everyone here is a strong counselor. Give yourselves a pat on the back. I'm sure we've all gotten bits of constructive criticism as well, but what I'm seeing is that everyone here has grown over the course of summers, and grown into really great leaders. Number two, and more importantly, this means we need to be pushing ourselves a little harder this summer to give purposeful, growth-oriented feedback.

"I have some ideas for how we're gonna accomplish this. First, I—along with Maria and the rest of the leadership team—want everyone to be able to give feedback to everyone. CITs and counselors, would you all do me a favor and raise your hand if you would feel comfortable, in the first week of camp, approaching your senior counselor with some growth feedback? Non-confrontationally, of course," Samira asked.

Nobody raised their hand.

"Okay. How about by the end of first session?"

Several hands lifted tentatively.

"End of summer?" Samira prodded.

A few more hands. But still, less than half the crowd had indicated that they'd feel comfortable calling a superior in on something. This was a problem.

Samira smiled again. Her grin was disarming. Even though Maria knew that Samira was just as disturbed as she was by this clear lack of a good feedback culture, one couldn't help but feel optimistic about their ability to solve even the most culturally ingrained problems when Samira looked so easily confident.

"CITs and counselors," Samira started again. "Do you all think that, in two or three years, when you all are senior counselors, that you will be perfect counselors who don't need any feedback?"

Without any prompting for volume or enthusiasm, the crowd declared, "No!"

"And, do you think that Maria, myself, Jamie, or anyone else on the leadership team sees as much of the senior coun-selors' actions as you all do, as the ones in the cabin with them?"

Again the crowd voiced their dissent.

"So, CITs and counselors, it's not only well within your rights—in the way we discussed on Monday, engaging around tension, not conflict—to give strong growth feedback to your senior counselors, because in a way, you all are the most qualified to give this feedback. Not us."

Samira paused to let this sink in, then swiveled to face the area where most of the senior counselors were sitting. "Like-wise, SCs, someone raise their hand and tell me who would help Maria grow if we weren't encouraged to provide growth feedback to others in the system, even if they technically out-rank us."

Ava volunteered. "Parents? On the surveys?"

Samira nodded. "Mm-hmm. Parents. Very true," she said. "Is that it?"

When nobody challenged her, she said, "That's not how Maria wants to operate, that's not how the rest of the leader-ship team wants to operate. If we wait until the end of summer to hear feedback from anyone other than each other, we'd never have the opportunity to practice and change." She spread her hands. "I rest my case. Questions?"

Nobody had any. Maria didn't know whether to interpret this as a good or bad sign. Naturally, she understood everything Samira was saying, but it wasn't clear whether the staff was just absorbing things, or whether this felt like too big or intimidating of an ask. She thought back to when she was a counselor at Starry Sky. She, clearly, had a great relationship with Robyn and Lane, even back then. But the thought of sticking up for herself, of marching up to a director and asking them to do something just a little bit better, would've still been terrifying.

"If I can jump in a bit here," Maria said. "Obviously feedback is important for all of us to be able to grow in the skills we need to be effective parts of this camp—team-building, collaborating, delegating, interacting with campers and each other. But feedback can also be something as simple as, 'Hey, Maria, I'm concerned about the staffing at skiing. I don't think we have enough people down there to keep the group safe, and I'm feeling overwhelmed. Would it be possible to schedule more people in the future if we continue to have signup numbers this high?' Then I'd go and talk to Laverne and see if we can switch some people around. Or, hey, I'll just go and help out myself if I can.

"This is sort of what we were trying to get across with the non-confrontational language stuff too, feedback is never an attack on someone's worth as a human," Maria continued. "I'm not going to feel threatened or disrespected if any of you come to me with a suggestion, or a piece of feedback, or a request for help. I want to know what I can be doing to better support you all, whether it's something as lofty as my leadership skills or as basic as where people are assigned during activities. So I'm actually asking you for this."

"Exactly right," Samira said. The staff was still silent, but their body language read as a little more sure. "So, now that we've talked about the benefits, and the need, for everyone to give feedback to everyone, I want to talk about what a good feedback session actually looks like. Let's think back to the scenario of a one-on-one sit-down with a senior counselor or someone on the leadership team."

Maria thought back to the first time she'd had a check-in as a counselor-in-training at Starry Sky. She and her senior counselor, Ella, were sitting on their beds in the counselor bedroom, facing each other. Their beds were the furthest two apart in the room, but nerves made Maria feel like the distance was much closer. Maria knew, logically, that she'd fulfilled the duties of a responsible and skillful counselor. She doubted that Ella was going to slam her over the head with a surprising piece of negative feedback.

Ella approached the meeting with an easy, genuine tone not unlike Samira's, but her use of the so-called "feedback sandwich," which is a bit of criticism bookended by glowing praise, had been prototypical and transparent. It wasn't a strategy that Maria endorsed now, as the director of her own camp. Even as a teenager, Maria had seen through it and, despite internalizing Ella's praise, mostly sat waiting for the negative "filling" of the sandwich.

See discussion activity 10.2 at the end of the chapter

The highlight of the meeting for Maria, though, had been when Ella asked Maria for her thoughts on anything that she could be doing better. Specifically, Ella had asked, "How can I support you more in what you're trying to learn this summer?"

Maria had been preparing for her senior counselor to ask for feedback in return and was racking her brain trying to think of something substantive. In truth, Ella was a fantastic senior counselor, warm and bubbly with the kids, not too demanding of her co-counselors. And she'd shown tremendous skill in resolving an ugly argument between bunkmates that had arisen within the first couple days. There was nothing that Ella was doing wrong, per se. Maria thought at the time that Ella was probably the best first senior counselor could have asked for, and she still believed it now.

But Ella hadn't asked Maria to tell her what she'd been doing wrong. She'd asked how she could be a better support for what Maria herself was trying to accomplish, how Maria was trying to grow. That was an easier question to answer.

"I don't feel like I can control a crowd," Maria had said.

"You seem like you're a natural."

Ella had laughed. "I'm definitely not, but I get what you're saying. We have a pretty rowdy group when they're all together in the cabin. It stresses me out too sometimes, but I fall back on experience."

"I wish I could just download your skills or something."

"Shame it doesn't work that way. Tell you what, how about you lead cabin cleanup tomorrow?"

Maria's hands gripped the comforter on her bed a little tighter. "Isn't that, like, senior counselor only?"

"Not necessarily."

Leading cabin cleanup entailed checking in with each of the campers and counselors to make sure that they'd done their tasks satisfactorily. On paper, it wasn't an especially difficult task, but it certainly necessitated a level of authority that Maria didn't feel she had. Cabin cleanup was a big deal at Starry Sky. Each cabin was scored each day by the cohort director. There were legitimately good prizes to be won—ice cream or pizza parties, an extra waterski session during free period—if a cabin had the highest score in their cohort multiple days in a row. Not only that, it was an excellent opportunity to build teamwork and camaraderie within the cabin, a daily group ritual before each camper went off on their disparate daily activities.

Maria's cabin was on a hot streak. They'd won their cohort two days in a row. One more would mean ice cream sandwiches delivered to their cabin during rest period. Maria was in awe of Ella's ability to build disciplined cleaning habits and accountability with the campers while still being, probably, the most well-liked counselor in the cabin. Just yesterday, the two campers who'd been in charge of the bathroom floor had been sent back to wrangle with the grimy floor twice before Ella pronounced it satisfactorily hygienic.

They'd complained each time, but the precedent had been set that cabin cleanup wasn't done until things were like new and ultimately they seemed to recognize that their hard work was worth it. After all, nobody wanted to live in a pigsty of a cabin, even if it was a pain to actually clean it as thoroughly as they did.

"We're about to win the ice cream party," Maria mumbled. "I wouldn't want to screw it up."

Ella chuckled. "Then don't. You know what the standard is. So do the kids. I have full faith in you to lead us to victory," she said magnanimously.

The next day, as the group crossed the threshold back into their cabin after breakfast, Ella told the campers that she had a meeting with Robyn and Lane she had to run to and that they should go to Maria when they finished their jobs, instead. Perhaps it was just the anxiety conjuring these visions in her head in the first place, but the jeering and eye-rolling that Maria had been expecting at this announcement never materialized. The campers snapped into action; pulling the sheets on their bed up tight, sweeping the floor free of the pale brown dirt that inevitably crept in from the camp grounds, straightening out their shelves, emptying the little black trash bin, and yes, scrubbing the accursed bathroom floor. The only difference was they came to Maria when they were done. The switch was so casual that a cohort director might have assumed she had been supervising cabin cleanup for the entire session.

Maria wasn't a more lenient supervisor than Ella, that day, either. Although she was a bit more cautious than Ella with her phrasing, who often dispensed a simple "nope" when a camper claimed to be finished with a task that had been done sloppily, Maria did send three campers back for another once-over of their shelf, another pass with the broom, a further smoothing of their sheets. Like Ella said, she knew the standard, knew how spotless their cabin would have to be to win for a third day straight.

So, after a few do-overs, Maria's cabin stood ready for the cohort director, Jonah, to march up to their doorstep and survey their work. When Maria, accompanied by Ella, saw him coming down the pathway from their neighboring cabin, she opened the screen door and held it for him, and walked with him as he did his slow, methodical sweep of every surface, every bed, every shelf. Ella, having swapped places with Maria for the day, stood with the campers in the center of the cabin.

"No notes," Jonah finally said, after he and Maria emerged from the bathroom. "Can't promise anything, but, on the eve of your possible ice cream party, this cabin has done what it would take. Well done."

Everyone in the room beamed. When Jonah left, campers and counselors alike erupted into cheering and clapping.

Ella approached Maria and said quietly, but earnestly, "Seems like you can lead a room just fine."

Looking back on it now, Maria was still in awe of both Ella and herself. Ella had done extraordinarily well to create a scenario where a CIT had felt comfortable asking for a leadership opportunity. Ella certainly hadn't been acting as a bad or unskilled counselor by withholding a cabin cleanup leadership opportunity from a first-year CIT for the first two weeks.

Maria had all but worshiped Ella from the start of camp onward. Had Maria been asked "Do you have any feedback for me?" she would have fallen silent for a good 10 seconds, hmmed, and said there was nothing, that Ella was pretty much a perfect counselor and that she was looking forward to the rest of the session, all of which was true, but none of which helped either of them grow.

And Maria herself had been brave and driven enough to reflect on her own strengths and weaknesses, even just two weeks into her first ever session as a counselor, and realize that she could still be a better front-of-the-room presence. She'd stood up for herself and asked, even directly, for an opportunity to lead. Or, at the very least, she'd asked for help.

Implicitly, this was feedback for Ella. Maria knew now that for the future of a camp, it is essential for senior counselors to step aside from time to time so their co-counselors can develop their own large-group leadership skills. Yes, they've earned their spot as the leader of a cabin. They've learned and grown and proven themselves through action and heart in their past several summers at camp. Now that they've attained the highest non-administrative position possible, it's their duty to train others. It wasn't an impeachment of Ella's character as a person or counselor that she hadn't done this so far. But now, sitting in the picnic area of her very own camp, Maria viewed that day as the start of her journey toward becoming a director.

Maria wondered if everyone else on the staff had conjured a memory as vivid as hers. She hoped that they'd been able to, though based on what people had said so far, it seemed like opportunities for feedback and growth as rich as what she and Ella had done for each other were rare here.

"A good feedback session isn't just about letting someone know they're doing something wrong," Samira said. "It's about that too, of course, but the real goal is to get them doing something more right. That's why sometimes the little things are the hardest to talk about. If someone was yelling at a kid, what would you do, as a senior counselor?"

Amused grins appeared on a few of the veteran faces in the crowd.

"Uh, is yelling at a kid a little thing?" Patrick asked seriously.

Maria knew that would cause a laugh and it did. She wanted to laugh, too, but it wasn't Patrick's fault. Samira had phrased the question interestingly.

"No, it's not a little thing!" Samira said. "Sorry, I should've made it clear I was going somewhere. No, yelling at a kid is a big thing, we don't yell at kids here. If it did happen, however, what would you do, as the feedback giver in this instance?"

Miguel was already speaking as his hand went into the air. "Tell them to get a grip," he said. Samira stared at him. "Non-confrontationally," he added hastily.

"Yeah," Samira said. "That's a big thing. You address that kindly, but firmly. What if, say, one of your co-counselors is

138   BLUE TRAIL BREAKTHROUGH

spending just a little too much time talking to another counselor when you all are together in the cabin when they really should be trying to hang out with the kids? Or maybe, if you're a CIT or a counselor, and you want to take on more responsibility but it seems like your senior counselor wants to do everything?"

Nobody spoke up, so Samira continued. "Neither of those last two things are fireable or disciplinary kind of offenses, at least not at first. Neither of those even mean, necessarily, that the person is a bad counselor. And this is the kind of scenario we encounter at camp most of the time." Samira began to pace in a slow circle. "I mean, I'm looking around at this group of people I've gotten to know a bit this week and I'm not seeing any bullies. I'm not seeing anyone who would just go and scream at a kid. Generally, we try not to hire those people." This got a big laugh, none bigger than from Jamie.

"But things still happen that need feedback," she continued. "Little things. Missteps and mistakes, not sins. So what do you do, as the feedback giver, whether you're a CIT or a senior counselor or the director? What do you do? How do you give that feedback?"

Brandon, a senior counselor who had stayed quiet for most of the week, offered to contribute. Maria sat up straighter. Most of the senior counselors, especially Miguel and Ava, had been eager to lend their voices to the group discussions throughout staff training, and Maria appreciated this. It benefitted the rest of the staff to hear from experienced voices who weren't on the leadership team. It lended legitimacy to what Maria, Samira, and the others were saying. But Brandon had refrained from exerting his presence in the large group. He always appeared engaged and Maria had overheard him giving some great advice when he'd led small groups, such as in the non-confrontational language exercise. He seemed to prefer to let the bigger personalities in the senior counselor cohort do the verbal annotating in the large group.

When he spoke now, it was clear and smooth, with hardly a pause or an 'um' to be heard.

"You just do," he said. "You go up to the person and tell them what you're seeing. Specifically. Maybe ask it in the form of a question, especially if they have more experience than you. You can say 'Hey, I noticed that you did this in this scenario, and I might've done it differently, but I'm curious about your approach. Do you feel comfortable sharing?' That's non-confrontational, too. Above all, give feedback in the way that you'd want it to be given to you. We all want to be good counselors. Part of that is being humble enough to take feedback, and gracious enough to know that when we receive feedback, it's not an attack. It's a chance to reflect and grow."

Patrick leaned forward to look across his row of seats at Brandon. "But how do you give feedback? Like, what do you actually say?"

Brandon smiled. "Correct me if I'm wrong, Samira, but I think this might be where this discussion is headed. There's no one way to give feedback. Or, at least, there's no script someone could hand you."

"Exactly right, Brandon, thank you," Samira said. "We've just laid out some guiding principles. Anyone got one?"

Patrick spoke up again. "Give feedback non-confrontationally."

"Mm-hmm," Samira said. "Very good. Another?"

"Everyone can give feedback to everyone," Miguel said.

"Yes indeed," Samira said. "And they need to. All right, there were a couple more."

"Feedback isn't just about things that are going horribly wrong," Lucy said.

Samira chuckled. "Very true, very true, constant feedback helps us prevent things from going horribly wrong. It can be for frequent things, common things, and it can also come in the form of requests. Things that people could be doing a little bit better to support others. One more guiding principle, who's got it?"

There were several seconds of silence. Maria suddenly imagined a test question in front of her; four blank lines, three of which had already been filled in. Even she didn't quite know what Samira was asking for.

Brandon did, though. "Be specific," he said, and Maria smiled to herself. She should've known it. Samira had talked about that very thing when she'd created her triangle diagram at the restaurant in Denver. "You can't act on feedback that isn't specific," he continued. "If you're going to make an ask of someone to do something better, it's best to have a concrete observation to share. And, better yet, maybe even a real suggestion on how to improve."

"Everyone hear that?" Samira asked. "I'd paint these four little things on the side of the dining hall if I could. One: Non-confrontational language; two: Everyone gives feedback to everyone; three: Feedback isn't just for disasters; and four: Be specific."

See discussion activity 10.3 at the end of the chapter

Maria thought back once again to her first time leading cabin cleanup. Her request of Ella fit into all four of Samira's principles for a good feedback culture. First off, Maria had certainly not accosted Ella for a more prominent role in cabin leadership. She had, however, even as a CIT, felt able and willing to give feedback to her senior counselor, even when nothing was going disastrously wrong. And she had been specific, not just declaring that she was feeling general malaise or lack of connection with the campers, but highlighting a personal area of growth that she thought Ella could help her with.

Maria loved the way that Samira had summed this all up. In the restaurant in Denver, she'd avoided getting too deep into the concept of "feedback," thinking that it was too big and too surprisingly difficult of a concept to distill into one dinner, especially when she had other triangles to cover. But Samira had just distilled it, for a crowd of teenagers, no less.

The Blue Trail staff looked attentive; eyes were locked onto Samira, side conversations were nonexistent. Maria dared to hope that today's talk had shaken off some of the counselors' notions of feedback—that a good feedback session could consist solely of "good work, I have nothing bad to say," that a CIT couldn't dare give feedback to a director, or that good feedback ever consisted of breaking someone down or "confronting" them.

If Blue Trail succeeded in stemming the outflow of campers and staff this summer, it would be thanks in large part to everyone holding each other to the common goals in just this way.

Discussion activity 10.1

Miguel's passion for rock climbing shines through and his focus on tracking progress is admirable. But he seems to have a very limited understanding of the range of ways in which campers can grow at climbing.

Think: While Miguel focuses on height and speed, what other aspects of climbing might Miguel suggest to campers as areas of growth? Consider technique, mental focus, balance, or even fear management.

Extend: SMART goals are Specific, Measurable, Achievable, Relevant, and Time-bound. In the case of climbing, instead of "climb higher," consider "master the crux move on route X within the next month." This is specific, measurable, achievable, relevant, and time-bound. Change gears for a moment to your workplace goals, how could you redefine them using the SMART format?

Discuss: Well-defined goals can often get lost due to the reality of the pace of work. How can you encourage your organization to not just set goals, but to track them in a visible and meaningful way?

Dissecting the Feedback Sandwich:

Think: Why might the feedback sandwich (compliment-criticism-compliment) be ineffective? Consider potential issues like inauthenticity, distraction, and demotivation.

Discuss: Share past experiences where receiving feedback in this format felt confusing, insincere, or unhelpful. Analyze what went wrong.

Consider: What negative consequences can the feedback sandwich have on individuals and teams? Explore issues like distrust, defensiveness, and missed opportunities for improvement.

Analyze: Identify specific examples of how this approach can hinder communication, engagement, and overall team performance.

Challenge: What are some effective alternatives to the "feedback sandwich" for providing constructive criticism? Consider clarity, specificity, and focusing on growth.

Discussion activity 10.3

Imagine the dining hall walls painted with these bold statements:

Non-confrontational language wins: Express feedback clearly and honestly, but with respect and kindness. It's about growth, not blame.

Feedback flows freely: Everyone, from intern to leader, has valuable insights to share. Speak up and lend your voice!

Celebrate the good, learn from the not-so-good: Feedback isn't reserved for disasters. Recognizing success fuels progress and even challenges offer opportunities to grow.

Specificity is key: Ditch vague comments. Point to concrete actions, observations, and suggestions for improvement. Make it clear what you see and how it can be even better.

Reflect: What might block you from embracing the above statements? What fears do you have? What skills do you still need to develop?

Think: What would this mean to you regarding the culture that would form if all of your co-workers embraced Samira's statements?

Commit: What specific actions can you take to embody these principles in your own interactions?

CHAPTER 11
FIVE WEEKS IN

YOU'VE gotta grab the rope," Jacob said over his shoulder to the camper in the water, a tiny 10-year-old who clearly hadn't tightened his life jacket enough. The straps were halfway up his face as he bobbed around trailing his two skis behind him, grasping fruitlessly for the ski rope.

"I can't get it fast enough with the skis on!" the camper, Mason, whined. "Can you come back around?"

Jacob thumped his fist against the steering wheel in frustration. He'd already looped the boat around one extra time to get the rope back to Mason.

"I'll come back around, but you gotta swim and grab it! Come on, dude, this is the easy part!" Jacob said.

"I'll try!" Mason said.

"Do more than try."

"Okay, I will!"

His voice was faint over the growl of the idling engine. It was the first ski period of the day. The sky was birds-egg blue, the water dark and smooth, undisturbed by the wind. Mason, apparently, hadn't gotten up at all in this first week of session two. He could sign up for skiing again next week if he really wanted to, but Maria knew how important it was—and how good it would make him feel—to get up today.

"Go easy on him," Maria said gently. "You're a pro. But you remember how hard it is to move around with a ski on your foot when you're first learning, don't you?"

"Yeah. Sorry. I just have a whole line of other people waiting to go," Jacob said.

"I have no doubt they'll get their turn. Just go easy on him," Maria said again. She lunged forward and grasped the rope in her hand, then swung her arm to flick the rope over to Mason. It landed perfectly in the crook of his neck.

"Oh, thank you!" Mason called.

"Thanks," Jacob grumbled as well. Then, as Mason was flailing about, getting his ski tips pointed in the right direction, Jacob shouted over his shoulder, "Knees bent, arms straight, stay in that ball. You're getting up today, I can feel it! The last few times have been so close!"

"Okay," Mason said.

Maria wasn't sure if he'd heard any of that, or if he believed it, but Maria did. This was not her first time observing skiing this summer, partly because it was an important and potentially risky activity, and partially because she liked riding on the boat and being there when campers accomplished their skiing goals. In all her previous times on the boat, she had found Jacob to be an exceptionally encouraging and competent instructor. She hoped that he would return next summer and, thankfully, he had expressed to her last week that he intended on doing so.

"Hit it when you're ready," Jacob said.

A few seconds passed. Mason was bobbing around behind the boat, but his ski tips were steady, a foot out of the water, slightly angled toward the boat. This was the best pre-start positioning of any attempt so far. Maria guessed he was taking a few deep breaths. That was always what she did when she was learning to ski. She'd never given an instant response when her driver asked her to give the "go" signal.

"Hit—hit it!" Mason said shakily.

Jacob pushed the throttle forward with practiced ease, not too slow as to drag Mason along but not too fast as to rip the handle out of Mason's small, ungloved hands. Mason's ski tips were drifting apart slowly, but, from what Maria could see through the churn of whitewater around Mason's skis, his body was rising out of the water.

"Knees bent, knees bent, knees bent," Jacob muttered. "Now get up!"

Mason's rear end was fully out of the water now and Maria could see his bewildered expression, his damp hair lifting off his forehead as the wind blasted his face. He was up, but caught in an awkward middle ground; knees bent too much, arms straight and pointed down toward the water. He'd spent the last week being told to hold his position, to let the boat pull him up, and now he didn't know what to do once the boat had done its job.

Jacob saw it too, glancing in the rearview mirror. "See if you can get him to stand up straight," Jacob said. He said it so quickly, the kind of thing he would ask of any spotter. But Maria was glad that he felt comfortable rattling off this request of her. The lake was his domain. She was on his boat. She'd gladly be of help.

She shifted off the comfortable bench seat and mirrored Mason's awkward posture, then lifted her arms to horizontal and extended her legs so her knees weren't bent quite so deeply. Mason hesitated at first, lifting his arms slightly before losing his balance a little and returning to his bent-over form. Maria repeated the movement. She would have yelled to him that he'd feel much steadier once he got into a good position, but there was no way she would be audible from this distance and with the engine now roaring.

Finally, Mason summoned the courage to raise his arms with more purpose. His body relaxed once he completed the motion. Looking at him now, it would be hard to believe that it was his first time skiing. Jacob's oft-repeated advice was to "sit back in the chair." Mason looked completely at ease now, as if he was lounging in a good chair in front of his television at home, watching a football game. His smile was as bright as the sun shining off the lake. Maria wasn't a huge skier, hadn't kept advancing after she learned how to slalom, but she still remembered the euphoria she'd felt when she'd gotten up on two skis for the first time. Even years later, the feeling was shockingly potent in her memory.

Mason's run didn't last long. After another 30 seconds or so, he slipped on a patch of rough water which had been generated by one of the other boats and pulled his arms towards his chest in an attempt to regain balance. This was the last thing that a skier ought to do to right themselves, and he fell backwards. His hand shot out of the water immediately—the critical 'I'm okay' signal—and Jacob pulled the boat around leisurely while Maria started pulling the rope in.

"You did it! How do you feel?" Jacob said, beaming at Mason.

"Good," Mason said, panting. "Really good. Finally got it."

"You looked amazing," Maria said. She vaulted over the engine cover and reached across the boat to grab Mason by the straps of his life jacket. This way, he could take off his skis without having to focus on keeping himself steady while he floated. The water was invigorating against her fingertips.

"I didn't think I was ever going to do it," Mason said.

"Why not?" Maria asked.

"I wasn't even close on any of my other tries, was I?"

"You definitely were close," Jacob said.

"Oh. Well, it didn't feel that way."

"Trust me, you've been getting closer all week. In my head, I was predicting you to get up today, and you proved me right."

Mason laughed. He had both his skis off now. He passed them up to Maria, who slid them along the inside edge of the boat. Moments later, he was back aboard, shivering slightly. Maria tossed him his towel.

"Did you get any pictures?" Mason asked.

"Oh, no, I didn't," Maria said. "I didn't know you wanted me to take any." The first couple of times she'd been on the boat, she'd whipped out her phone to take pictures and videos of campers, in the hopes that she'd capture their first time getting up. Then a few of them had told her to put the phone down after she'd gotten several faceplants on video. After that, Maria had respected the performance anxiety.

"Sign up again next week and we'll get all the video you want," Jacob said cheerfully. "I'm proud of you, bud."

He brought the boat back up to skiing speed to take them back to the docks. Mason dismounted, as did Maria, wanting to socialize with the campers who were still waiting, and to help keep things orderly. She noticed that the line of campers was becoming more of a blob, a blob which was starting to inch into the area that they needed to keep clear for boarding and exiting boats.

It was nearing the end of the first week of session two, and Maria had already accomplished her goal of learning every camper in this new session's name. Starry Sky also operated on a schedule of two sessions of four weeks each, but there were always many more two-session campers at Starry Sky than there were at Blue Trail this summer. Even among the older cabins, the age groups less likely to be homesick after four weeks, less than a third of campers remained in camp from the first session. So she still had many names to learn and was proud of herself for once again being intentional about seeking out interaction with every camper. She hoped that all of the counselors were doing the same. In her experience, this point in the summer—the end of the first week of the second session—was where burnout ran rampant.

See discussion activity 11.1 at the end of the chapter

She didn't want to assume a crisis of energy among the Blue Trail staff, but Jacob's little bit of grumpiness on the boat with the rope was another small piece of evidence toward a conclusion that the staff, as a whole, was starting to fade. Had it ruined Mason's skiing experience? Probably not, that little retort was surely overshadowed by the monumental achievement of getting up for the first time. Maria flicked a glance over at Mason now, standing with his friends who had yet to take their ski runs, bouncing excitedly while still wrapped in his towel. He certainly looked happy.

Yesterday, while she was observing baseball during second period, a conflict had broken out between two campers after one slid into home and insisted he was safe, despite clear evidence to the contrary. The baseball director, Nolan, had made the correct ruling, but when doing so, told both campers to "shut up" and threatened to make them both run a lap around the field if they couldn't cease their hostilities. Maria had spoken with him afterward and he was apologetic, but she was shocked that it had happened in the first place. Nolan had been nothing but soft-spoken and kind during staff training.

Later, during the "capture the flag" game, several counselors who were supposed to be playing defense had been standing huddled near their team's flag, talking about what they were going to do on their night off. At Starry Sky, Robyn and Lane had always maintained that counselors should never betray any desire to be anywhere other than camp when they were around campers. Maria didn't list it as one of her biggest pet peeves, but she could see why this behavior always made Robyn and Lane so upset. Campers knew that nights and days off existed, of course, but it could still sting to know that their counselors were counting the minutes until they could be away from them. So it had taken a fair bit of restraint on her part to make sure she addressed the situation while maintaining her own patience. Luckily, by this point in the summer, people were indeed in the habit of asking each other to "teg" (tension-engage/grow) as a form of hashing things out, so she'd leaned on that to talk with the counselors as visions of Robyn and Lane's serious faces flashed in her mind. And, though this was the first year she'd collected data, Maria did notice that the average cabin cleanup score for the first week of session one was markedly higher than for the first week of session two. All evidence that, as a whole, the counselors were struggling.

When skiing was over, she said goodbye to Jacob and walked back up the path toward the camp office, hoping that Jamie or Samira would be in the building. They both were. It was a slow morning, she supposed. Samira was standing by the coffee maker pouring a container of creamer into her steaming Blue Trail mug. Jamie was reclining in his old brown leather desk chair, picking placidly at the guitar he used for campfires. They both tensed a little at her arrival, realizing that this picture probably didn't look incredibly productive to their boss, but at this point in the summer, Maria was very happy with the way that they'd gelled as a leadership team. She understood that not everybody had to attend to something pressing at every moment in the camp day. The only thing Maria was annoyed about was that Jamie was playing her least favorite campfire tune.

"Can I hit 'skip' on this song?" she asked.

"I already tried," Samira said.

"We can hit pause," Jamie said. "Something on your mind?" He set the guitar down on the floor so that it was leaned up against his desk.

Maria sat down in her own chair and wheeled it out into the center of the room. The three of them shared this front room of the office. Nico had a separate office in what was basically a glorified shed closer to the picnic area. Stu and Laverne also shared an office down the hall, though Laverne was rarely there, as she mostly spent her days sitting in on the various activities in camp. There was a spacious extra room that was probably meant to be Maria's office, but the previous director had apparently used it for a meeting space, or a room for people to talk privately with campers or counselors who were having a hard time. Maria decided not to reclaim it as her own space.

Besides, she liked being in the same space as Jamie and Samira. The three of them had gotten to be quite close. She was pleased to say that she knew much more about Jamie than she did at the start of summer. He was in an alt-rock band back home. He didn't have roommates or a significant other; he lived with only his dog, Penny, who also accompanied him to camp every summer. He was also allergic to coffee, which tugged at the heartstrings of Maria and Samira, both coffee enthusiasts.

"Have you all noticed people seeming pretty burnt out this week?"

"A little," Samira said. "But week five burnout is common. They gave their session one campers everything they had to offer, and now those campers are gone and they're still here."

"Yeah, I mean, I get it," Maria said. "But I'm getting a little more concerned about it."

"Did something happen?" Jamie asked.

"A few little things." Maria told them about skiing, and baseball, and capture the flag, and a couple of other interactions she was pretty sure wouldn't have happened during session one. These were exactly the kind of things they'd talked about during Samira's discussion of feedback, nothing fireable, nothing that put anyone's emotional or physical safety in serious peril, but things that were below the standard they wanted to set as Blue Trail leaders.

"What do you want to do about it?" Samira asked.

"At our senior counselor meeting tomorrow, let's do a temperature check. See how everyone's feeling," Maria said. "I'd love to be wrong, I obviously don't want there to be mass burnout on staff, but I think that's what we're seeing. Like you said, pretty normal, but still something we have to nip in the bud."

"Agreed," Samira said.

"I'm happy to lead off the discussion, but if one of you really wants to," Maria trailed off. Samira had done well checking in on and establishing good relationships with the counselors all summer long, making good on her desire to take ownership of more responsibilities. And campers and counselors alike flocked to Jamie wherever he went. His natural charisma was undeniable and people always felt like he was on their team. Maria felt good about the relationships she had built with the staff. She had made it a priority to create meaningful ones. But she had to recognize that, while she would of course participate in the discussion, there were others on the leadership team who probably had more pull with the staff as a motivator.

"They hang on to your every word," Samira said to Jamie.

"I was about to say the same of you," he replied.

"You're the Blue Trail legend, Jamie," Samira said. Then, looking at Maria, "I mean, do we need to decide this now? We're all gonna be there."

"I guess not, I just didn't know if either of you had anything you really wanted to say."

Jamie scooted his chair forward and knit his hands on his desk. "I can—I mean, I can do it if you want me to." He appeared fascinated with the faux-wood grain of his desk.

"Are you sure?" Maria asked him. She and Samira caught each other's eyes.

"I can do it, I just need a little more information about what you're observing."

Maria didn't quite know what he meant. She'd already laid out the skiing grumpiness, the baseball argument, the capture the flag laziness ... if he'd asked her two weeks ago to list out any instances of burnout she'd seen, she would have been hard-pressed to find one. First session had, by and large, been an exemplary four weeks in terms of counselor enthusiasm, skill, and professionalism. She'd even gone out of her way to commend Jamie in a recent leadership team meeting for hiring an outstanding staff.

"I don't think there's anything beyond what I've already shared," Maria said. She was glad Samira's desk was on the other side of Jamie's, the social worker had just issued a mighty wince. "I just think that what I've seen this week could get worse if we don't say something to the tune of, 'Let's get focused up again, we know it's five weeks in, but you've all been doing great and we want to keep it that way.'"

"Yeah, of course," Jamie said. "Unless you think the staff would think it's a little vague. I'm worried it could come across as too hard on them one week into session two."

"I understand the worry," Maria said. "I'm definitely not trying to be too hard on them, but I don't think this is. Nobody's in trouble; we just need to re-check ourselves. And we'll be specific, without calling anyone out, of course, but I wouldn't just come out and say, 'Hey, do better.'"

"If you already have an idea for what you think should be said, maybe you should kick off the talk," Jamie said.

Maria briefly debated pressing the issue. While Jamie's tone hadn't been unkind, Maria didn't feel that she'd been at all unclear with what she'd been observing from the staff over the last week, and she didn't think that Jamie was being entirely genuine with his "confusion" over what to say. Samira was right, they were all going to be there, it really wasn't a big deal who made the opening remarks at their senior counselor meeting. And maybe it was a mistake for Maria to turn that into a big question, but she hadn't expected there to be any tension. Now she was definitely in need of a teg with him.

She decided to relent for now, though. "Yeah, okay, that sounds good, unless you wanted to do it, Samira," Maria said.

"All you," Samira responded. Once again, Maria felt like she could communicate telepathically with her. Samira was wearing her signature look of benign bemusement, the look Maria had seen many times when Samira was getting ready to gently guide someone to a major course correction.

They dropped the issue until after lunch. The midday meal for today was pizza and salad, which always served to further lift people's spirits, even if most of the campers completely avoided the salad. Maria chatted contentedly with Laverne and Nico. Jamie sat at the other end of the directors' table, which Maria tried not to read as a sign of avoidance.

They hadn't fallen into a regular seating arrangement, even after five weeks, and there were only eight of them at the table—the six members of the leadership team, plus the two health center nurses. It would be hard to avoid someone at the directors' table, even if one wanted to

Maria had learned one good thing that happened this week: More people had signed up for the first slate of trips than last session, which had already been an improvement over session two of the previous summer. Nico was doing a remarkable job building on his good work last summer, and Maria was pleased to hear that the bulk of the increase in signups had indeed come from the younger cabins, the very campers they'd talked about getting more involved in trips in their very first meeting back in February.

After lunch, when the campers and counselors had retired to their cabins for rest period, Maria asked Jamie if they could talk for a moment outside the office.

They stood together in the shade of one of the maple trees that hung over the office building.

"In our conversation earlier about the senior counselor meeting tomorrow, it seemed like you were a little uncomfortable. I'd love to hear more about how you felt, if you're open to sharing," Maria said.

Jamie crossed his arms and smiled. "Is this a teg?"

"I would like it to be," Maria said seriously.

His smile disappeared. She didn't want to seem intimidating, but the rational part of her brain was good and loud; Jamie's response this morning to a pretty simple request and observation had been strange. She was modeling effective leadership by re-addressing it quickly and professionally.

"I was confused when you expressed that talking to the counselors today might be too demanding of them. It didn't really seem like you were on board with it."

"I am on board," Jamie replied. "I just don't know why you made a big deal about who's 'leading off' the discussion."

"If it came across as me trying to unnecessarily choreograph the meeting, I'm sorry. That definitely wasn't the intention. On the other hand, now I'm kind of glad I asked. The intention was to give you space to work your magic; what Samira said is true, they love you. But, instead, I felt invalidated, which was surprising, because one of the issues I brought up, the baseball thing, was something that I remember you talking about in one of our meetings before the summer. A counselor resolves a disagreement, but in a way that comes off as abrasive and doesn't make the kids feel heard. You said you had dealt with this before."

"I deal with it in the moment," Jamie said. "From my point of view, if it's a quick thing like that, you just address it right then and move on."

"I did address it then, this is what I'm saying, it's part of a pattern," Maria replied. "Yes, it's quick, as in it's not something anybody is going to get fired over. I do think it's these kinds of moments where we get the most growth. Where we push them just a little harder than they're used to, and they become better leaders because of it."

Jamie pursed his lips for a second. "What happened during 'capture the flag' again?"

"We had counselors talking about how excited they were about their nights off while campers were in earshot."

"Yeah, that's not great," Jamie admitted.

"Okay, then I'm really not sure I understand. It seems like we're in agreement that morale is seeming kind of low."

"Sure, but I think we're only going to lower it more by getting in their grill."

"There's no getting in anyone's grill, Jamie, this is just a recalibration. And if you don't want to say much during the meeting, that's fine, but my bigger concern now is whether you're on board with what we talked about during staff training and before the summer."

"You really doubt that I'm on board? After the session one we had?"

"Yeah, session one was amazing. The staff hit a groove, the campers had a blast. That was then. The staff is getting tired now. Things are getting tougher. Frankly, this is how camps lose people. They don't support counselors with the little things, so there's no opportunity to grow, so it's either a fun time with no substance, or something bigger happens and they get spooked by it."

"Maria, it's going to be okay," Jamie said.

She hadn't been expecting him to say something so simple. It took the next words out of her mouth. On one hand, she was still angry with him. He still seemed reluctant to do a pretty simple course correction with the counselors. On the other hand, she found herself involuntarily calmed by the confidence with which he'd spoken. Maybe she was indeed overreacting.

Then she thought back to Robyn and Lane. They were always vigilant. They stepped up in the big moments and the small ones. Their jobs were hard; they asked a lot of themselves and others. And Starry Sky was a great camp because of it. Maria took another moment to center herself. Things were indeed going to be okay—not because that was just how things naturally were—things would be okay because the team would take action to ensure that.

"This isn't the kind of thing we can let slide anymore," she said. "We agreed on that before the summer. If this kind of talk is going to be difficult for you, it's going to be an issue."

Jamie looked positively pained. He was leaning against the maple tree, looking at the ground. She'd never seen him like this before. He'd been such a big part of creating so much meaning for everyone at camp this summer: leading campfires, making every kid he talked to feel special, fostering close relationships among the staff. But, when it came time to address a drop in the quality of counseling over the last week, he wilted.

"I just don't want them to hate me," Jamie muttered.

Maria exhaled through her nose. Something else her former mentors had shared came rushing back through her mind. Their former assistant director, JT, had been loved by the counselors, the parents, and the campers alike. In the end, however, they'd let him go. When the tougher moments came, he had not been able to hold himself or others accountable. Every camp has a JT, Lane had said. It appeared that Maria had found hers.

She had no doubt that Jamie was a compassionate man and a virtuoso when it came to relating to campers and staff alike. Maria also knew that he loved camp with all of his heart, but now she knew one other thing: His need to be liked was in danger of interfering with the respect that he'd already earned. Yes, he loved camp, but he, more than anyone else on the leadership team, really needed to feel that love in return. And that would hold him back from being a truly effective leader as long as he continued to view a good working relationship as one that never involved a hard conversation. She wanted to give him this chance, at their upcoming meeting, to prove that he could hold people accountable. If he continued to shrink from this all-important aspect of leadership, however, his future at Blue Trail was very much in doubt.

What Maria had told Robyn and Lane was true, though; she still did not want to lose anyone this summer.

"They won't hate you," Maria reassured him. "They really do love you. They respect you. They need to hear this from you. I'm not asking you to tell them that they're horrible counselors. I'm asking you to get everyone back on track toward our goals. I know that you've done it before and I'm asking you to do it again, now."

The encouragement drew his eyes back to meeting hers. "I hear you," he said. "I can do it. I know this is a place I myself need to grow. But I'll do it."

See discussion activity 11.2 at the end of the chapter

Discussion activity 11.1

Navigating Predictable Moments in Staff Culture

Discuss: Share experiences where staff morale dipped at predictable points in the annual or seasonal cycle? What could have been done differently?

Analyze: Brainstorm specific challenges staff might face during these periods and their potential impact on engagement and well-being.

Plan Ahead: Map out proactive leadership behaviors and support strategies to address anticipated challenges during each identified period. Include items such as increased communication, team-building activities, or workload adjustments.

Discussion activity 11.2

The Price of Silence: Addressing Tough Issues in Group Dynamics
Jamie's desire to avoid directly addressing the observed poor counseling raises questions about the potential impact on group dynamics and staff morale.

Think: How important is trust and open communication within a team, especially in a leadership role like a camp director? How can a leader balance support and accountability?

Discuss: Share experiences where leaders directly addressed problems within your team. How did it impact trust, communication, and overall team dynamics?

Challenge: Imagine you witness a colleague behaving poorly but your leader avoids addressing it directly. How would it make you feel? Would it affect your trust in the leader and your confidence in the team?

Ripple Effects: Examine the broader impact of a leader's communication choices beyond the immediate situation. Evaluate how open dialogue and proactive engagement could positively influence staff morale, clarify expectations, and foster a culture of proactive problem-solving.

CHAPTER 12

NOTICING

S O that's it, really," Jamie said. "We know that everyone is exhausted and that it takes a lot—a lot—of energy to bring it 100 percent every day at camp. But let's just take this moment, at the end of week five, to recommit ourselves to making this place the best it can be. To not just keep things calm and going as they'll go, but to create magic for this new group of campers. This is such a meaningful experience for them and we get to help create that meaning. So, let's do it. Sound good?"

The "Yeah" Jamie got in response from the group of senior counselors was muted, but resolute. Miguel looked especially determined, his eyes dark, sitting forward with his elbows on his knees.

Despite Jamie's promise, Maria had not gone into the meeting expecting him to speak much. He had proved her wrong quickly, not steamrolling her or Samira by any means, but addressing the talented crop of senior counselors with equal measures of compassion and directness. Combined, they'd only stayed on the topic for a few minutes and as Maria met the eyes of a few of the SCs, she felt like the leadership team's message had landed. These were small, yet critical aspirations that a healthy staff should always be ready to agree to. Choosing to be more compassionate, more patient, more energetic in those little moments where it would be so easy to just solve the problem with maximum efficiency — these were the marks of great counselors.

Maria sat back and allowed herself to breathe quietly for a moment while Samira guided the group into the next phase of the meeting. She'd been dreading tonight, but Jamie had risen to the occasion, and because the leadership team was united, there was nothing controversial about their message. She was very glad he'd stepped up. Since he was so passionate about all things camp normally, his absence from the discussion would have been noticed. It might have even felt like a quiet protest.

The rest of the agenda for the meeting was fairly simple, much like the agenda for the four previous senior counselor meetings they'd conducted this summer. Each meeting opened with the leadership team bringing concerns or announcements to the forefront, then individual SCs could address items that they'd added to the agenda. For instance, in their meeting before Bluelympics, Blue Trail's all-camp competition day, Miguel had implored the other senior counselors to "turn the energy way up, for the next 24 hours you act like you're playing in the Super Bowl."

Then, they went around to each of the senior counselors to check in on how their cabins were meshing. Most of the time, each counselor had at least one concern of substance to address. Like most issues that arise at camp, it usually wasn't anything catastrophic. But the senior counselor meeting was a great place to source ideas from the leadership team and the other SCs, who were likely experiencing some of the same highs and lows.

Sometimes, however, a counselor didn't produce anything substantive when it was their turn to share. There were always a few who said something along the lines of "it's been a good week" or "no crises." But, this summer especially, the leadership team was trying to push back on those kind of responses. Maria trusted the senior counselors enough to believe they weren't hiding anything when they did this and she knew that some counselors were just naturally concise and unfussy individuals. They didn't feel the need to take up time in the meeting if there wasn't anything hugely problematic to report.

Maria always thought back to her first feedback session when she was a CIT in Ella's cabin back at Starry Sky. There were no crises there either, but if Maria had simply strung a few one-word responses together, if she'd foregone the opportunity to lead cabin cleanup, it's possible she wouldn't be the leader she was today. So, she and Jamie, Samira, and even Stu or Nico or Laverne, when counselors said things that related to their arenas, always asked follow-up questions, always pushed counselors to strive for more than a crisis-free environment. Maria was glad to see that other senior counselors had also taken up this task. If anything, they asked follow-up questions even more gracefully than the leadership team did. Whenever an SC asked a follow-up, it came across as genuine curiosity about how their friends were doing with their cabins, not as a boss probing for subtle issues.

Samira was doing this now with Brandon. Maria respected him greatly and she knew he had really smart things to say when he was pushed to say them and campers really seemed to enjoy him. A good camp staff couldn't consist solely of extroverts who were great at getting campers riled up for whatever activity was happening. Campers, like any other humans, craved conversation and connection as well. And Brandon was great at making campers feel valued as whole human beings. But he did tend to offer very little verbal contribution in meetings.

"I'm glad nothing crazy is going down in cabin six," Samira said. "It's been a week, do you feel like people are connecting with each other? Are you seeing anyone that seems left out?"

"People seem to be vibing," Brandon said. "Half our cabin knows each other from past summers, so they seem to have picked up where they left off."

"What about the other half?" Jamie asked. "Are the experienced kids reaching out to them? Including them?"

"There haven't been any fights or breakdowns or anything. I don't know whether I'd say that the experienced kids are, like, reaching out, but I'm not seeing any signs of real exclusion or anything."

"Okay," Jamie said. "I mean, it happens, kids who know each other are gonna stick together."

Maria jumped in. "Yes, obviously friend groups are friend groups. We're not going to discourage existing friendships from continuing. We also need to make sure that new campers feel included." She didn't want to pick on Brandon, but even if there would naturally be kids who were already familiar with each other in every cabin except their youngest, it was important to her that all campers made new connections each summer. "Brandon, I'm curious, would you say that every camper in the cabin has found at least one other camper that they regularly talk to?"

"Yes, mostly," Brandon said. "There are a couple who like to read on their beds during rest period. It's hard to tell whether that's because they really want to or because they don't feel comfortable inserting themselves into some of the little pods that already exist."

"It would be valuable if you were to find that out," Maria said. "I'd like everyone to do this for their cabins, not just Brandon. We're a week in, this is the perfect time for you all to really notice the dynamics of your cabins, or your activities. Notice who's sitting and reading. Notice who's lingering by a conversation but not talking. Notice who comes alive during a game but doesn't talk to anyone after. Find out whether people are connecting. Brandon, let's use your cabin group as an example, if you don't mind?"

"Please," he said.

"Well, I'm imagining Brandon or the other counselors in his cabin could lead a game in the next couple days. Or find a fun group challenge that's not cabin cleanup. That offers opportunities for people to break out of their usual dynamics, opportunities to work with new people and see everyone's fun sides. And, I'll be curious, when you do that, notice what happens."

"I thought you were going to pick on me a little harder than that," Brandon said.

Maria grinned. "I'm glad you didn't feel exposed. Who can see themselves trying that with their cabin groups this week?"

Some staff hands raised.

"Another great thing to do is to ask those quieter kids if there's anything that they really want to do or play that they haven't done yet," Miguel chimed in. "Or even whether they do feel like they've made a good friend yet." Maria noticed that, as always, the other SCs leaned a bit more forward when he spoke than when any of the leadership team members did.

"Great idea, Miguel," Samira said. "One, it shows those campers that you see them and you care about them, and two, it gives you some intel about how they like to shine, and helps them connect more comfortably when the activity is right up their alley. The quiet kid who's really good at kickball isn't going to come alive if you have a cabin-wide lanyard-making session."

Maria laughed and it brought back another memory of Starry Sky, this time from her first year as a senior counselor. There was a camper in her cabin, named Hailey, who was on the autism spectrum. Maria had looked over her medical file and talked to her parents before the session started and they'd shared with her both on paper and over the phone that Hailey had a lot of trouble initiating conversation with peers. At school, Hailey would often tell teachers that she was perfectly fine sitting or doing an activity on her own, but then would come home and speak of loneliness.

Six days into that session, it seemed that the pattern was holding. Maria herself had made a great connection with Hailey; they had a common interest in video games and had both brought stuffed Nintendo characters to camp. But Hailey struggled to hold an extended conversation with any of the other campers in the cabin. Maria regretted not being more proactive sooner, but she wanted to see if Hailey could push herself in this new setting before interceding.

That afternoon, during free period, Maria had gone back to the cabin to use the bathroom only to find Hailey sitting on her bunk, playing with some light-blue slime. Hailey often had slime in her hands. Although she had made the batch she was holding now in arts and crafts earlier in the week, she'd also brought her own pink-and-purple batch from home. She'd given it to Maria once, just to feel. Maria was no slime expert, but she could see why turning the glue concoction over in her hands over and over was relaxing for Hailey. The slime was fairly bright when it caught the light and Hailey had added little white pellets, almost like styrofoam shavings, to the mixture to give the slime some more texture.

"Can I sit with you?" Maria asked.

"Yes," Hailey said.

Maria sat next to her. Without Maria asking, without Maria even thinking to ask, Hailey handed her the slime. Maria smiled and emulated the movements of Hailey's hands—squeezing, pulling, kneading.

"How's this week been for you?" Maria asked.

There was silence for a few seconds before Hailey answered. This too was common and Maria had learned to just wait patiently, not to repeat herself or assume that Hailey hadn't heard.

"It's been good," Hailey said.

"What's been your favorite part?"

"Arts and crafts. And the campfire last night."

"Yeah? I'm glad you liked it. I like the campfires too."

"Yeah, the songs were really funny. The one about the bird especially."

Hailey's parents had also said that she didn't love loud singing and that campfires might pose a challenge for her. Indeed, Hailey had started the campfire hanging back in the outermost ring of bleachers, but over the course of the evening she'd worked her way in until she was all the way at the front, where she had to squint her eyes to protect from the smoke and the brightness of the fire.

"Do you think you've made some good connections with some of the other people in the cabin?" Maria asked.

"Maybe," Hailey said. "I don't know."

"Anyone?" Maria asked.

Hailey considered. "Aimee. And Noelle. They're nice, they're in arts and crafts with me."

"Do you all talk when you're at arts and crafts?"

"Yeah, but not here. Here they're always talking with Britt and Jimena."

School style superlatives didn't always map precisely onto the dynamics of a camp, but these four girls that Hailey mentioned were the closest thing in Maria's cabin to the "popular girls." They were all very sweet kids, but when the four of them were together, they barely paid attention to anything except each other. Maria could see why Hailey—or anyone, for that matter—would have trouble making inroads with that friend group, even if she already seemed to have a friendly relationship with Aimee and Noelle outside the cabin.

Maria squeezed the slime firmly, feeling it ooze up between her fingers. Then she had an idea.

"I think it would be fun if we made slime as a cabin sometime," Maria said. "I could go and get the supplies from the arts and crafts hut. It's just glue, activator, baking soda, and food coloring, right?"

"Yeah," Hailey said. "Do you know how to make it?"

"I'm gonna guess you just mix all that stuff together?"

"Yes, but you have to have the right amount of each."

"Well, I'm clueless about that," Maria said cheekily. "Maybe you should show everyone."

Hailey fell silent again. Her eyes were fixed on the small wooden table in the middle of the cabin, upon which the remnants of a chess game and a couple dented and sticker-adorned thermal water bottles stood still.

"I guess I could do it," Hailey said.

"Only if you think it would be fun. No pressure. But you're clearly a master of slime-making and I think it would be cool for everyone else to learn from you."

At this, Hailey smiled, just a little. After a shorter silence, she said, "Okay. I'll do it."

A few days later, when the cabin was all together during rest period, campers and counselors alike sat on the floor with paper mixing bowls in front of them and followed Hailey as she instructed them on how to make the perfect slime. Throughout the session, most of the campers, including Aimee and Noelle, checked with Hailey to see whether they were adding the right amounts of glue and activator, or whether they liked their concoction. The first few times Hailey had been asked a question, she'd looked at Maria and Maria had gently prompted her to answer. Once Hailey realized that this was truly her show, she became a very encouraging and engaged instructor, dispensing compliments and advice with a bubbly energy that Maria hadn't seen from her so far this session. After everyone finished making their slime, Maria was overjoyed to see Hailey sitting on Aimee's bunk, chatting with her and Noelle like they had been tight all summer.

The slime workshop wasn't a magical solution to Hailey's social anxiety and difficulty initiating, nor did Maria expect it to be. Hailey still had her quiet moments over the course of the summer, but Maria did notice that the others in the cabin sought conversation with Hailey more often after they'd all created a space where she could shine. It was hard to be a new camper. As welcoming as Starry Sky prided itself on being, there were so many traditions and existing relationships and daily rhythms that a first-timer had to navigate. For someone such as Hailey, who already spent a lot of time alone during the school year, the new environment of camp was even more daunting. Thankfully, a good counselor noticed who was likely to hang at the margins of the spaces they were charged with creating and sought ways to make sure everyone felt included and appreciated.

At the end of the summer at Starry Sky, campers received little scrapbooks with printed photos that the camp photographer had taken of them. On the last page of these scrapbooks, there was a page for each camper to write down the answers to some questions about their summer:

My favorite activity was _____. *I went on* ___ *(#) trips. My favorite camp meal was* _____. The last question on this last page was, *My best friends at camp were* _____.

Experienced counselors knew that they'd done well in creating a close-knit cabin when they saw that campers were struggling to fit the names of all of their "best friends" onto this one small line.

It was traditional for people to sign the inside back cover of each others' scrapbooks, and when Hailey gave hers to Maria to sign, Maria could see that Hailey had indeed written down Aimee and Noelle as her best friends at camp. Even more pleasing was when the two other girls turned over their scrapbooks for Maria's signature and she saw that they had also written Hailey's name down on the line. True, they had written down almost everyone in the cabin, along with half a dozen other campers, so they might have interpreted the term "best friends" a little generously, but they'd still thought of Hailey when asked to think of the people they'd connected with most over the summer. Maria knew that if Hailey's parents could've seen that page in their books, they would've been ecstatic that they'd decided to send Hailey to Starry Sky that summer.

Maria told this story now, in the senior counselor meeting and the group had their eyes on her the whole time. She found herself moving her hands more than she usually did when she spoke, as if she was still toying with the slime Hailey had let her hold. This kind of noticing, Maria thought, was what truly separated great counselors from good counselors. Having a likable, charismatic personality, or being able to project one's voice enough to lead a game, or even being able to resolve a camper conflict—these were important skills, and crucial to creating a fun and safe camp culture. Like Maria, Samira, and the rest of the team had been preaching all summer, the real art of camp work came in the subtler moments. A master counselor didn't just defuse the most intense conflicts when they arose. They noticed the social dynamics in their cabin early on, worked with their co-counselors and camp leaders to navigate them, and created a space where every camper could feel loved and included for who they were.

"So, notice," Maria said. "We're five weeks in. We're all tired. But keep coming to these meetings with everything. Look for the little issues, the little dynamics, and bring them up here. You are all brilliant, dedicated people. Like Jamie said, let's keep working together and creating the best camp possible for everyone here."

Ava initiated some snaps, which gave the group a chance to signal their warm assent. Miguel was nodding vigorously.

Maria smiled. "Who's up next?"

CHAPTER 13

AFTER SUMMER ONE

MARIA couldn't see much of anything outside the windows of the dining hall. The sun was an hour gone now and the trees had become murky shadows against the charcoal sky. There was the dirt of the Picnic Area, illuminated in faint orange from the few lights they had on over the benches. A dark mass was all Maria could make out of the office building. It took the absence of campers and staff to realize just how remote Blue Trail really was, deep in the woods. Maria had never been one for personifying nature, really, but she imagined now that, if she were a Blue Trail tree, she'd be relieved to rest in a quieter space, eager for the last of the people of Blue Trail to head into their winter hibernation elsewhere.

The leadership team, however, had some final business to attend to, here at their usual haunt, the directors' table.

Maria had taken the liberty of making a pot of hot chocolate and everyone sipped delicately from camp mugs as Stu distributed a stapled packet of papers to everyone. These were the collected results from the all-important end-of-summer surveys. Within the packets, there were photocopies of campers' responses, written in the sloppy handwriting of kids who'd gone weeks without school.

There were also comments from the staff, which Maria was anxious to read. After a bit of a burned out start to the second session, the staff had responded well to the leadership team's call to action and over the course of the last three weeks of camp, Maria had observed too many instances of exceptional counseling to recount. While there were still some issues, she would gladly take this staff as a whole back for another summer and desperately hoped that the surveys would indicate the same sentiment from the counselors themselves.

And, of course, there were the insight-generating parent responses. A 3.8 out of 5—that was the score parents had collectively given last year to the likelihood of their children returning to Blue Trail. That number had hung over Maria's head all summer as an inspiration. It felt dramatic to pin the future of Blue Trail to just one number, but if one had to pick a number that could predict the camp's fate, it would be that one. It had to be higher.

"Let's, um, let's start with the campers?" Maria prompted. There was a tinge of fear in her voice. She didn't want it there, but with one summer having gone by with this team, she didn't feel the need to hide it either.

"Looks like most of the stuff we were already doing well, we are still doing well," Stu said. "First and foremost, 80 percent of campers strongly agreed with the statement 'I had a lot of fun this summer,' and another 10 percent, er, normal agreed."

"Okay, that's really good!" Maria said. As they'd framed out during staff training, however, fun was a low bar for a meaningful camp experience.

"That's a pretty standard number," Jamie said. "Happy to see it, for sure, but I don't think we should be surprised."

"Yeah, I'm not surprised, but I think it's a more important stat than normal for this summer, since we did shake things up and get more serious with having our instructors actually instruct," Laverne said.

"Right," Stu said. "The usual thought is that instruction is inversely related to fun, but we approached the summer testing the hypothesis that kids would experience more impact growing better at the things that they want to get better at—and it would still be fun. It seems we've proven ourselves right."

"Good job, us," Maria said, grinning. "I'll definitely take those numbers staying at the standard when we made such a shift in style this summer."

Stu had even more to report.

"Another nice thing, 85 percent of campers agreed or strongly agreed with the statement 'I had at least one person in my cabin who I now think of as a close friend,'"

"Woo!" Jamie exclaimed. "That's a big one. That's what we want to hear."

That number didn't jump off the page to Maria as being particularly great. "How does that compare to last year, Stu, do you know?"

"It's higher," he said. "A good bit higher."

Maria was a little surprised that it wasn't even higher than eighty-five. In her view, the senior counselor meetings had been more and more productive over the course of the summer. People really had been sharing out the little things, the subtler dynamics. It felt like the senior counselors had really tried to notice who was feeling included and who was hanging at the fringes of their cabins. While Maria was glad to see improvement, she knew the people who did not agree with that statement were probably the newest campers; the ones who hadn't come into the summer with pre-existing friendships. These were the campers who they really needed to stick around in order to boost their enrollment and if that large of a percentage of them didn't feel like they'd made inroads, it was a problem.

"What are everyone's thoughts on this number?" Maria asked, attempting to project neutrality.

"I like that it's higher," Nico said. "But it doesn't seem great; more than one in ten of our campers can't say that they had a close friend at camp by the end of the summer? That's disappointing. Like, we really tried."

"Yeah, I'm surprised," Samira said. "I mean, think about it; that means there's a camper or two in every cabin who felt like they didn't have a good friend in camp. We probably didn't broadcast the 'noticing' mentality strongly enough. "

"Or early enough," Maria said.

"But, we totally had the 'what makes a good counselor' part of staff training," Jamie said.

"Well, it seems like that didn't quite do the trick," Laverne injected. Maria looked at her. "But I think it's a necessary part of staff training, of course."

"Maybe we need to make it more explicit that this is one of the most important things a counselor can do," Maria said, more gently. "Look out for cabin dynamics and do everything they can to make sure that number is as close as possible to 100 percent." She flipped through her packet of tables and charts. "Stu, do we have any data on the split between first session and second session for this question?"

"I can dig it out later," Stu said. "I didn't filter for that when I was arranging this packet."

"I think it'd be important to see. If you could gather that data, that would be great."

Nico took a dramatic sip from his hot chocolate, which Maria guessed was now simply warm chocolate. "I have a thought," he said. "And this could be way off, because it's largely based on my camp experience, which wasn't the best when I was actually in camp—"

"I'd say we're in need of a conversation with someone who had a less rosy perspective on camp," Laverne said bluntly.

Nico shrugged. "One of the reasons I gravitated toward trips so much was because I came into Blue Trail later than most of my usual cabin mates and I never felt like I got super close with them. On trips, however, you bond really quickly with the people you're with. There's automatically a common interest there, and share growth. I always felt like my cabin mates were who I was supposed to be bonding with, but they were never really my closest friends."

"Were you ever in a cabin with Miguel?" Maria asked.

"Nope," Nico answered. "But we both liked climbing and we both liked trips. We always had to go our separate ways at the end of the day and during rest period, so it wasn't until we both became counselors when I felt like, 'oh yeah, this can be my guy.'"

"I'm not trying to deny your experience, Nico," Jamie said. "But do we really think that many people just aren't meshing with their cabins?"

Everyone was trying to interpret the data and figure the way to the kernel of truth.

Maria wondered whether Nico's experience was truly the average for campers who weren't Blue Trail lifer, and she wanted to hear more. She was also conscious of the fact that one thing Jamie took pride in was being a "glue guy." He could create a game in any scenario at a moment's notice. Chemistry and fun were considered his specialties and he spent a great deal of time in staff training beseeching counselors to focus on creating fun times within their cabins, even though most of a camper's day would be spent away from their cabin mates. It was possible that even though he'd shown tremendous growth himself this summer, Jamie still interpreted that 85 percent as somewhat of a personal slight.

"I'm just offering a theory," Nico said, raising his hands. "Not saying I'm the template for all campers ever, but I do think that cabins can get pretty cliquey. And we can never have enough emphasis on teaching counselors to facilitate new relationships."

Maria grabbed a Blue Trail pen from the pile that was strewn out over the center of the table. She flipped her packet over onto its blank backside and scribbled a note.

They worked through the rest of the camper data, and Maria was relieved to see that they had maintained or improved on their scores from last summer in all of the safety areas. Blue Trail campers felt physically safe and emotionally cared for. And, crucially, 95 percent of campers agreed or strongly agreed with the statement "I loved my counselors this summer." Even if there were clearly some things the leadership team needed to lean on more during staff training, that figure brought a huge smile to Maria's face. It meant, generally speaking, that the staff Blue Trail had recruited for the summer was warm, fun, and engaged. They had the dispositions to succeed as counselors and the finer arts of leadership—team-building, bringing people in, delegating, conflict resolution—could be taught.

Finally, they arrived at the camper data point Maria was most interested in. They'd been very intentional about their phrasing on each survey, asking similar questions in different ways for campers, counselors and parents. Everyone on the leadership team knew that campers could be very introspective when given the right prompts. Samira and Laverne's experience working in schools had come in handy when designing the camper surveys. And because growth could be an abstract concept, they'd end up splitting the growth question that would be posed to counselors and parents into two questions for campers: "Did you get better at things you were interested in this summer?" and "Do you feel like you learned something new about yourself this summer?'

"Eighty-six percent," Stu said slowly, looking around the table at each member of the leadership team. "Eighty-six percent of campers said they got better at something they were interested in."

"Wow," Jamie said.

"Now that's huge," Samira said.

Even Laverne had a big smile on her face. "Credit where credit's due, Jamie. Glad we didn't do a whole overhaul on how we hire people."

Jamie laughed. "Don't give me the credit. We all pushed our staff to take more ownership of their activities and these numbers show that they took that message to heart."

"I agree," Maria said. "I'm so grateful for all of you and the staff. We should share this with them, somehow. They need to know their hard work paid off."

Everyone nodded. "What about the second part of the growth question?" Maria asked.

Stu took a beat before responding. He was looking at her gravely. Maria braced herself.

"Eighty-nine," Stu said, his face lifting up into a smile.

"Let's go!" Nico enthused.

"God, why were you looking at me like that, Stu?" Maria said, leaning forward onto her hands. Her shoulders shook with gentle laughter.

"You're not in the mood for a bit of dramatic flair?" he raised one eyebrow.

"This is really good, though," Maria said. "Especially since the way we asked the question was deliberately open. 'Learning something new about yourself' could mean so many things for so many different people. It could be overcoming a fear, discovering a new interest, learning what you look for in a friend, learning how to make friends."

"Camp gives you what you need the most," Samira said, smiling at Maria.

All of these incredible results made the one sub-optimal number—the one-in-ten campers who said they didn't have any close friends by the end of summer—that much more perplexing. But it was also energizing. There had been so many questions at the beginning of the summer. What would the staff be like? How would the leadership team gel? How could they stem the outflow of campers and counselors alike? Could Blue Trail regain its former prestige? And Maria supposed some of these questions would arise each summer. Based on the camper surveys, they'd made progress on some of the more essential questions, and there was now a clearer roadmap to continued success at the camp.

"I remember what it was like picking my kids up from the airport when they came home from camp every summer," Laverne said. "They always had so much to say. Talked my ears off in the car ride home, and over dinner, and until they zonked out. I loved hearing everything. I have a feeling that parents heard a lot of good things about this summer."

"I hope you're right," Maria said. "I bet you are. Do we want to look at the counselor surveys first, though? Unless anyone has anything else to say about the camper data right now?"

They all examined the next several pages of the packet. Stu had extracted several written responses to go with the tables and numbers here and Maria's eyes pored hungrily over each paragraph. Although, from a financial perspective, Blue Trail's future depended on parents' decisions, the counselors' feedback was intriguing to Maria. Like campers, they were living in the cabins, present for activities, building meaningful friendships, and creating the distinct energy of this particular summer at Blue Trail. Unlike parents, the counselors were also acutely aware of the actions of the leadership team. They had a broader perspective than almost anyone else in the ecosystem of camp.

So far, most of what Maria was seeing was a relief, where 95 percent of counselors had agreed or strongly agreed with the statement, "I had fun on staff this summer," and 80 percent with the statement, "By the end of the summer, I had someone on staff that I would consider a close friend." Another 95 percent indicated that they felt "supported by the leadership team." Similarly high figures said they were satisfied with the amount of time off they had, and that they were comfortable bringing up tension with either their co-counselors or the leadership team. Maria was especially pleased with that last bit—they had spent so much time during staff training imploring the staff to be honest with each other, to shed their fears over the idea of feedback.

Based on the data, and on Maria's experience working with this wonderful staff over the summer, the teaching had eventually sunk in. Maria knew this to be true not only because the line on the counselor survey indicated as such, but because the full picture of the data set was looking so positive. So far, what they'd seen was the picture of a successful summer. And successful summers did not happen without strong cultures of feedback.

Naturally, Maria's mind jumped to the small number of counselors who didn't agree with these statements. She had a good idea who they were; with counselors, those who felt disconnected from the rest of the staff tended to be those who struggled the most with the actual duties of counseling. They'd made it through the summer without firing anyone, but there had been a few tough conversations. A few private "call-ins," as Samira liked to refer to them, to avoid using the term "call-outs." Maria knew that perfection wasn't a realistic goal; not for the campers, not for the leadership team, and not for the counselors. As she looked over the data, she started to blame herself more and more for every figure that wasn't 100 percent positive.

See discussion activity 13.1 at the end of the chapter

"Here's something interesting," Nico said. He rapped the edge of his packet on the wooden tabletop. "Only around 60 percent of the counselors thought they 'learned skills that are applicable to other jobs and settings' this summer."

"That's puzzling," Samira said. "Especially considering the good marks for all the stuff that, well, concerns those skills."

"I agree, Samira," Maria said. "I mean, they said they felt comfortable giving feedback—that's a skill. They said they had fun and made friends—in a camp context, that's team-building, and that's a skill. Even the bit about time off—recharging, time management, those are skills!"

"I totally agree," Samira said.

"I will say this makes me pretty concerned," Jamie said gravely. "All the other numbers are great, but if people aren't thinking that being a camp counselor does anything for them except teach them how to be a camp counselor, that's not good. That doesn't cut it for people when they get to be around college age. That's when the idea of spending your summer in the woods becomes a bit of a tougher sell."

"Maybe it was just the phrasing of the question," Laverne

said. "Like you said, this is the only not-great mark we've gotten from the counselors so far."

"That's true, but I think we have to note this," Jamie said, leaning forward.

Maria had things to add, but she sat quietly. This was growth from Jamie. He was pushing the leadership team to do more, to do better. He wasn't content, as he had been since Maria had come to know him, to simply let the status quo continue, even though the status quo afforded him a position of great popularity and respect. The Jamie of a few months ago, or even a few weeks ago, wouldn't have shown so much concern over this one mediocre figure. That Jamie wouldn't have thought twice about 40 percent of counselors thinking that camp counseling and scooping ice cream, for instance, didn't have any overlapping skills. This Jamie was a new, more reflective, stronger leader.

"The things that we teach here are necessary in any kind of job that anyone could have," Jamie said. "Accountability, trust, communication, focus ..."

"Those triangles," Nico said, smiling.

"Yeah, those triangles," Jamie confirmed. "You talk to any employer on the face of the plane, and they're going to want someone who has mastered those qualities. They may phrase it differently, sure, and the application will look different in every context. Focus on camp counseling is different than a focus on scooping ice cream, but it is still focus. And if the value of focus—and accountability, and trust, and communication, and everything else we teach—isn't coming across at camp, then it's going to be hard for them to fall back on it when they do land that prize internship in a field they are hoping for.

"This is not a stretch; it's our lived experience," Jamie continued. "I know there's a reason why most of us have been in the camping world for, like, decades. Most of our staff will not go on to careers at a camp; but while we have them and they are devoting their energy and their precious summer time to us, we need to make it clear that the qualities we ask for them to display are essential for anything they want to do later on. And it would be huge if more than 60 percent of our staff agreed with that."

"Thank you for saying that, Jamie," Maria said. "I think you're absolutely right. Like all of us, I think, I'm a little surprised at this feedback, but let's use that shock to think about next summer. What can we express differently, in our recruitment process, articulate during staff training, and make very clear over the summer itself, to convince a larger percentage of our staff that they weren't just "spending their summer at camp"? That they were here learning skills that they'd be hard-pressed to learn anywhere else at this point in their lives? That these skills will make them more effective in their careers and more marketable to employers? How can we name and celebrate those skills?"

"It's the same way we talked about fun in staff training," Laverne said. "We pitch Blue Trail to counselors as a fun summer in the woods, playing games with kids and working with people their age. We thought that what appeals to counselors about camp is that it's not serious. And of course, a camp job is more fun than some office internship or whatever. But parts of camp are pretty serious, and they teach real skills, and I think we've been underestimating how much potential counselors, especially the older ones who are going to be looking at internships as well, want that. So let's sell that. Plus the fun stuff."

With that, they moved to the final section of the feedback packet: the parent data. Maria's hands shook slightly as she turned the pages. She hated how nervous this was making her. She had been there this summer, and by and large, it had surpassed her wildest hopes. As with any summer, there were things to improve. But Maria felt prouder now than she had after any summer in her life. Her experience and the on-paper evidence buoyed that feeling.

For ease of comparison to the data from last summer—the data they'd shared with the counselors during staff training—Stu had compiled this year's number into the exact same style of table, with last summer's numbers in parentheses.

My child was physically safe and secure.	4.9 (4.8)
My child was emotionally safe and secure.	4.4 (4.2)
My child had a lot of fun.	4.7 (4.7)
My child had meaningful relationships with peers	4.4 (4.2)
My child created meaningful relationships with adults.	4.8 (4.3)

"Only one score changed more than a couple tenths from last year," Nico noted.

"But it's the one that had the second-highest correlation with likelihood of return," Stu said.

"Let's key in on that word 'meaningful,'" Maria said. "While we didn't ask parents whether their kid liked their counselors, activity leaders, or even us directors, but based on the high marks in the first three categories, we can pretty safely assume that we hired a staff that our people generally liked. We did ask whether the relationship was meaningful. Meaningful relationships help you change as a person. That's where the increase is coming from. This summer, in the same way we went beyond having activities that are just fun, we also went beyond just having a staff that is liked."

"Well, on the subject of growth…" Samira started.

Maria's eyes dropped back to the paper.

My child grew in a noticeable way over summer (e.g., emotional intelligence, leadership and team-work skills, activity related skills).	4.7 (4.0)

"Oh," Maria said. "Oh my gosh, that's . . . "

"That's what we wanted," Jamie said, with a relieved laugh. "That was the whole goal."

Maria was beaming. She took a celebratory swig of hot chocolate, relieved that it had now cooled to lukewarm, though she probably wouldn't have cared if it was still hot. These numbers weren't perfect. She would have really liked to see significant increases in the peer relationships and emotional safety categories, and the lack thereof probably had something to do with the counselors' obvious struggles to fully pick up on the social dynamics of their cabins. But everything else had either been a very high mark or a substantial improvement, and their score had skyrocketed in the very category that was most closely correlated with retention.

So, it was no surprise to Maria when she found the next line in the table read:

My child plans to return to Blue Trail next summer.	4.5 (3.8)

Maria met Stu's eyes and they were crinkled with delight. In that moment, he reminded her a lot of Lane. They didn't look a lot alike, but, like Lane, Stu had supported Maria at every turn. He'd been nothing but reliable and cheery and welcoming the entire summer.

"You've been sitting on that number this entire time," Maria said to him. "Jerk."

"I mean, we had other important data to process as well," Stu said. "I knew that once we got to this part, the celebration would commence."

"I can go grab some stuff from the minifridge," Laverne said slyly, starting to rise from the bench.

"Well, okay, yes, we should," Maria said. "But first, we gotta talk about one more thing." Laverne sat down again, raising her hands.

Maria took a breath. "Needless to say, this is amazing growth and I'm so proud of all of us and our staff for making it happen this summer. On a more personal note, I was pretty terrified coming into this summer. It was natural, I guess, but still."

"Yeah, it was your first summer directing, that's totally understandable," Jamie said. "Obviously you were more than qualified and you've proven that time and time again, but there's no scenario where running a camp for the first time isn't nerve wracking."

"Exactly," Maria said, smiling at him. "The nerves were definitely wracked. But you all have been the best team. Unbelievable. I kind of just want to fast forward to next summer already."

"I'm good without the fast-forward," Samira said. "Breaks are good."

"Fair," Maria replied. "I hope you have your usual very relaxing year in your job as a school counselor."

Everyone broke out in laughter, which made the dining hall feel a little larger. For a fleeting moment, the sound was not unlike when campers filled the long benches. Then it died down, and the strange emptiness, the darkness of the woods outside the windows, returned.

"Well, the last thing I wanted to get to and then we can call it a night," Maria started.

"Or commence the festivities," Laverne said.

"Or that," Maria chuckled. "But I wanted to bring back our triangle model." She flipped her packet over and drew out the familiar four-triangle shape, writing" accountability," "trust," and "communication" in the outer three triangles and "focus" in the central one.

"This summer, we chose to focus on focus," Maria said. "We had one goal, which was to retain campers and staff. The last several summers had seen a sharp decline in enrollment, and we needed to reverse that trend, or else Blue Trail would have to change pretty significantly in order to stay afloat." Everyone was nodding. They knew this story. They'd all been breathing it for the better part of the last year.

"Well, we won't know for sure until people sign up or apply for next summer," Maria continued, "but based on what parents said in the survey, and our ability to recruit new people, we should be very optimistic about an increase in both campers and staff.

"I think, because of that, we can switch the triangles around, if you will. Of course we always want to have a clear goal, of course we always want everyone focused on that goal. But, unless there's a shocking disparity between the intention that parents expressed to have their kids return, and what we see during signups, our goal for next summer doesn't have to be so existential. Do you all agree?"

"Yes. I don't want to jinx us," Samira said. She rapped her knuckles on the wooden tabletop. "But I think you're right. I also think that, despite all the glowing numbers, there's definitely stuff for us to improve for next summer."

"Seems like most of the areas in which we faltered centered around emotional safety. Inclusivity. Facilitating connections among campers," Stu said. "I'd argue that's communication."

"I second that," Nico said. "And we did a pretty good job over the summer getting into those hard conversations when necessary. Not saying we don't need to worry about accountability, but it doesn't need to be suddenly plopped into the center."

"Right, Nico," Maria said. "And, yeah, just because something's not in the center definitely doesn't mean we just forget about it." Accountability hadn't been their central priority, but Maria still managed to tension-engage a lot of people this summer, including everyone on the leadership team.

"I also think it should be communication in the center," Samira said. "Not just having better relational communication in the cabins but better and earlier growth communication between us and the counselors."

"One hundred percent," Maria said. "Laverne? Jamie?"

"Communication is great with me," Laverne said.

"Same. And, like we've talked about, there's so much overlap between all of these," Jamie added. "You train your attention on one, you lift up all the others, too. Even if we could have done better creating emotional bonds among some of the campers, I think our growth communication, mainly with the campers, was surely better than years prior. Look at how many parents say their kids grew this summer."

"That's true, too," Maria said. "Just because we're moving a triangle into the center doesn't mean that we've been completely failing to uphold it. Seems like we're all in agreement about communication, then. Over the coming months, we'll brainstorm specific ways that we can be better support for the staff and the campers. As for now," Maria set her pen down and stood up, "I think it's time to crack open the mini-fridge."

"Hear, hear," Jamie said, placing a hand on Nico's shoulder and giving it a playful shake.

The leadership team settled into easy conversation as Maria strode toward the dining hall doors. They were already starting to reminisce over funny stories from the summer, stories which Maria was now part of. She looked up at the rafters, the thick horizontal beams upon which framed picture after framed picture hung. In each picture there were hundreds of campers and dozens of staff members. And there were over a hundred photos ringing the dining hall, over fifty years' worth of sessions. The picture quality improved, the faces changed, growing older, popping in and out as people came and left, and sometimes came back and left again. Finally, Maria got to this summer's pictures. She and the leadership team stood at the center of the back row in each one. She liked how small she was in these pictures, how even now, even after she'd looked at them several times since their hanging, it took a few seconds for her eyes to find herself. She was only a small part of this community, really; just one person, one reason this summer had been so meaningful.

She was proud and excited to hold that same spot in many, many more pictures to come.

She stepped outside the dining hall, then slowly through the picnic area, her feet crunching too loudly over the gravelly dirt, despite her best efforts to walk quietly in the night. She continued past the trees, the brown of their bark barely discernible under the dim lights, and into the office building, which was finally tidied up, now that the leadership team could take their time and process the summer.

The minifridge was down the hall, in the cozy room they used as a meeting space. But Maria took a moment to sit down at her desk, leaning all the way back into her chair. Her gaze drifted to the ceiling, and she stayed that way for a long minute.

She didn't want to keep the others waiting too long for refreshments, but there was one thing she had to do now that she was alone and had cell reception.

She drew her phone out of her pocket and opened her text thread with Robyn and Lane. All those months ago in their house in Tucson, they'd vowed to always be a support for Maria, and they'd kept that promise. Their text thread was full of long messages from each of them—wisdom, ideas, stories, and struggles. It was a virtual, typed-out reconstruction of the kind of meetings that had taken place every day at Starry Sky, the kind of meetings Maria was leading herself now.

She slowly typed out a message, deleted it all, then typed it out again. The requisite words to express her gratitude were difficult to find, but she did find them, and after the message was delivered, she took another moment to sit down comfortably at her desk. There were no tasks left to do, except grab some bottles from the fridge and celebrate with her new camp family.

Discussion activity 13.1

Calling In vs. Calling Out

Discuss: Share examples of situations where someone was "called in" vs. "called out." What were the key differences in approach and outcome?

The Power of "In": Analyze the core elements of calling in: empathy, respect, focus on growth, and offering support. How does this create a safe space for learning and improvement?

The Impact of "Out": Consider the potential drawbacks of calling out: shame, defensiveness and damage to trust and relationships. Explore how it might hinder open communication and collaboration.

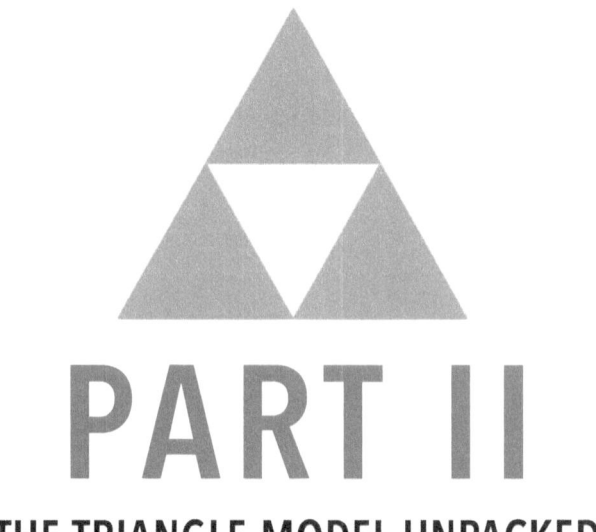

PART II

THE TRIANGLE MODEL UNPACKED

DURING the ACA conference, Maria and the Blue Trail team discuss a theory of effective teamwork that we've affectionately named the Triangle Model. As Samira outlined, the model consists of four adjacent triangles representing four characteristics of high performing teams: **focus, communication, accountability and trust**. At the intersections of these triangles lie additional behaviors, depending on which of the four triangles a team chooses to prioritize.

For the Blue Trail team, which lacks overt toxicity but also lacked a clear direction to stem their loss of campers and staff, finding and maintaining a unified **focus** was their priority for the summer. As a team, they chose to focus on creating an environment that promoted technical and social-emotional growth for campers and staff alike.

They restructured activities to be more instructive, trained their staff to give and receive feedback non-confrontationally and proactively, and pushed their counselors to be more observant of cabin dynamics. And due to the team's new focus, on their end-of-summer surveys, more parents reported a desire to send their children back to Blue Trail the following year.

For your team, your priority—the center triangle—may need to be something else. Do team members avoid owning up to mistakes? Do they let tasks slip under the rug until a superior notices that something is going awry? If so, **accountability** likely needs to take center stage.

Do team members often report confusion on instructions or goals? Is there a scarcity of chemistry within the group? The main issue is probably **communication**.

Are there open lines of feedback between leaders and staff? Do staff members tell leaders when something isn't working for them? If the answers to these questions are "No," then the work environment may lack **trust**.

Choosing a center triangle should not be a unilateral decision. It's likely that a discussion on which of the four triangles to prioritize will illuminate other areas of growth for your team. The issue threatening Blue Trail's livelihood was so clear that almost everyone on the team agreed to lock in on whatever it took to promote retention. But, as we saw toward the end of the book, there were indeed some issues with trust. Jamie displayed a difficulty in trusting that fairly simple feedback would be received well by the counselors. There were lapses in communication. Maria doesn't follow up Samira's apparent desire for more responsibility until Samira pulls her aside at the ACA conference. Before the summer began, Laverne reported that holding activity leaders accountable to the ostensible goals of their activities, which was instruction, had been difficult. Blue Trail had growth opportunities to address in all four triangles. So, too, does every organization.

Overall, though, they agreed that what they needed was a new focus. The status quo wasn't working for the camp and they needed to change course. It is possible, even probable, that members of your team who work in different arenas could have very different ideas of what the central triangle needs to be. Embrace the multilateral aspect of the central triangle decision, agree on a priority that the whole team feels motivated toward, and remember that just because one triangle is in the center, it doesn't mean that the other three fall to the wayside. Successful teams work continually on all four, or else their ability to support and engage with tension — the big band encircling the whole model — is weakened. With that, we give you the full triangle model, complete with each triangle's intersections.

FOCUS

"Everyone on the team agrees on their goal, works collaboratively toward that goal by using an agreed upon roadmap, adapts to challenges that arise, and pays attention to the results of their efforts."

Think of a focus as the application of your organization's mission statement. *Why* does a camp such as Blue Trail offer the things that it offers? Maria and Laverne touched on this during staff training, when they talked with the staff about "fun" being a low bar for a meaningful camp experience. Once the leadership team at Blue Trail decided that their focus was creating an environment that enabled growth, it infused everything they did with a new sense of purpose. An activity leader for basketball can feel right in making their campers shoot free throws every day — not simply because they, on a whim, think that's good practice, but because it's the camp-wide focus to help kids learn new skills.

A unified focus also promotes collaboration over conflict. For instance, recall the argument between Jamie and Laverne over hiring for personality versus skills. When the point of contention was initially raised, Jamie presented as defensive and Laverne as bitter. They had been operating with no focus for the last several years, so it really was a conflict between two people with competing visions for the camp. But, with Blue Trail's growth focus, the tension was not around whose vision was "best" or, even worse, who had more sway. Rather, it was about how to change up hiring to actualize the focus on growth, and the answer ended up being somewhere in the middle of both viewpoints. Hiring remained largely the same, per Jamie's wishes, but Laverne gained more agency in asking for more from her activity leaders.

Attentiveness to results is another behavior of teams with good focus. For as much as the Blue Trail team talked about emotions before and during the summer, they always had their eyes and minds on the hard data of the parent surveys. They cared about whether all the changes they made amounted to an improvement on the all-important question of "My child plans to return to Blue Trail next summer." The focus for the summer was determined using data, and the focus for next summer will be determined using data. Feedback items from parents, staff, and campers are not just "problems to address," they are direct indicators of how well your mission statement is being actualized.

Intersection #F1: Focus x Communication → **Clarity**

Teams without clarity meander in their communication and actions. They restrain themselves from saying what needs to be said. They over explain, while simultaneously under inform. The end result is confusion on goals, tasks and feelings.

On teams with clarity, however, each member is clear on exactly what needs to be happening every day, what their goals are, and what needs to change, if anything, in their performance. Clarity leads to proactivity, which is people taking initiative on their goals rather than waiting to be instructed or reminded. There are no secrets on a team with clarity. No secret goals, which will rupture focus, and no secret feelings, which will break trust and cause paranoia.

Intersection #F2 Focus x Accountability → **Responsibility**

Responsibility refers to the obligation and willingness to take ownership of one's actions, decisions and outcomes. Whereas others can hold a person accountable, responsibility is a person's own internal drive to be a successful member of the team. A responsible team member ensures that their goals are met and their commitments fulfilled. They understand that the focus of the team cannot be achieved without their individual contributions.

Stu exhibited a good sense of responsibility during the Blue Trail team's early discussion on challenges they faced in the past. He indicated that it was often difficult to stay entirely in the loop on how individual campers were faring, and that sometimes he found himself in awkward situations with parents because of that gap in knowledge. Although he devised a system that worked better for this summer, he also took responsibility for not taking ownership on this issue in the past. A responsible team member should think, "What do I need to do to advance our unified focus today? How am I going to make sure that it gets done?"

Intersection #F3 Focus x Trust → Alignment

Alignment refers to the state of having shared goals, clear direction, and a mutual understanding of priorities and objectives within a team or organization. It involves ensuring that everyone is on the same page and working together toward a common purpose, fostering trust and maintaining focus.

Alignment is less of a behavior than a culture. When a team is in alignment, everyone trusts that everyone else is doing what they need to do to advance shared goals. Organizational leaders can spend less time supervising and more time coaching, or building chemistry. Leaders who are aligned with their staff feel less stress, and staff who are aligned with their leaders feel less surveilled. When feedback occurs within teams that are aligned, it is not a fear-inducing event. Tweaks to behavior can and should still be made when necessary, but it is all in the name of realigning toward that unified focus.

ACCOUNTABILITY

"Good accountability means that one, I do what I say I'm going to do; two, you do what you say you're going to do; and three, we all help each other do what we're supposed to

*do to meet our goals. If one of us doesn't live up to the
expectations, we take it upon ourselves to 'call them in' for
an opportunity to grow and make it right."*

The concept of accountability is often discussed in a
judicial, punitive light. It doesn't have to be this way. You
may be familiar with the idea of "high support, high
accountability." When organizations have built a culture that
prioritizes both support and accountability, they find they
have a supportive atmosphere that includes a drive for
excellence. They are willing to take risks and learn from their
mistakes. Constructive feedback is welcomed and acted
upon.

On these teams, however, the goals are set as a group,
drawn from the expertise of people in various departments.
Everyone is accountable to that shared goal. Yes, Maria has
the power to make changes to the leadership team. But the
fact that they all agreed to a goal before the summer began
meant that each member was accountable to a vision, in
addition to their supervisor. Moments of accountability, then,
are truly opportunities for individual and collective growth,
rather than punishment.

Even in what might have been the most tense moment in
the story—Jamie hesitating to call in the counselors in week
five—Maria does not vocally threaten to dismiss him if he
doesn't come around to her "side." She reminds him that the
leadership team committed to giving counselors feedback
even if—*especially* if—the mistakes they were making were
not fireable. The behaviors that Maria wanted to address had
been seen by every member of the leadership team, this
summer and in past summers. Part of their vision was to not
let these behaviors slide. With some encouragement, Jamie is
able to reorient himself toward this shared vision and become
a more ego-free leader in the process.

Every organization has a vision for what they want to
accomplish. Every organization employs human beings who
will make mistakes along the way. What separates a
successful organization from an unsuccessful one is how well

its members hold themselves and each other accountable to that vision.

Intersection #A1: Accountability x Focus → **Responsibility**

Please refer to Intersection #F2 earlier in this section.

Intersection #A2: Accountability x Communication → **Transparency**

Transparency refers to the practice of openly sharing information, decisions and actions, in a clear and accessible manner. It involves honest and frequent communication within an organization, as well as being accountable for one's actions and decisions. Organizations that lack transparency are rife with gossip and unhealthy speculation about the actions of leaders and workers alike. Workers should know why they are being asked to practice certain behaviors, or the rationale behind the decisions that leaders make.

Transparency is especially important in organizations that employ high numbers of young people, such as camps. Young people are especially perceptive and sensitive to things like hypocrisy, dishonesty and overburdening. They should be looped in on the mission of their organization and understand how their responsibilities contribute to that vision.

Blue Trail's staff training is not just about what to do if a camper skins their knee, or how to drive a boat. The leadership theory that Maria and the team discuss in the offseason gets relayed to the staff once everyone convenes at camp. They are not just workers, but developing leaders, and organizational transparency is critical for helping young people buy in to the responsibilities of their positions.

Intersection #A3: Accountability x Trust → **Integrity**

Integrity refers to the alignment of one's actions, decisions and behaviors with ethical principles and values. It involves being honest, reliable and consistent in one's actions, thereby building trust and fostering accountability.

On paper, integrity is one of the most easily understood traits a successful organization can have. Members should take ownership of their responsibilities and areas of growth. They should not gossip or throw others under the bus. They should hold themselves to a high level of moral character, especially in youth-led organizations like camps. Campers do inherit behavior from counselors, younger counselors from older counselors, and older counselors from leaders. Everyone in the organization should be able to see their supervisors conducting themselves positively, honestly and ethically.

Organizations that cannot boast this characteristic will function as a collection of disconnected individuals who are afraid to take ownership of their actions out of a mistrust of others' reactions. And none of the leadership theories outlined above can take effect without the bare minimum of employees who conduct themselves with integrity.

COMMUNICATION

"There are three kinds of communication that happen in a workplace and can accomplish goals: relational communication, task communication, and growth communication."

This breakdown of communication into three distinct flavors is not arbitrary; similar to the triangle model as a whole, organizations can be skilled in one or two forms of communication, but lag in another, and the whole workplace could suffer as a result.

For example, a workplace that has chemistry (relational communication) and is able to exchange feedback effectively (growth communication) can still find itself having to give more feedback than it should because the deadlines, action items and responsibilities (task communications) are unclear for its members.

Blue Trail had things to work on in all three areas of communication. Thin task communication reflected the aforementioned lack of focus: activity leaders didn't know their true responsibilities. On one hand, there were few examples of true discord among the Blue Trail leaders, but on the other, Maria admits to knowing precious little about her coworkers, even after several offseason meetings. She attempts to rectify this lapse in relational communication once she gets to camp and meets the entire staff. And, of course, counselors, campers, and parents didn't feel that Blue Trail was offering valuable skills training, which speaks to a real lack of growth communication.

Although it is possible for a breakdown in one form of communication to hamper others, it is likewise possible for an improvement in one facet to aid others. A rising tide can indeed lift all boats. Team members who genuinely like and respect their coworkers are more likely to feel secure in seeking clarification on tasks and far more likely to show the vulnerability and open reflection needed for growth. Organizations that invest time and thought into clearly communicating tasks, rather than seeming clinical, facilitate a calmer environment that aids in team chemistry. And task communication applies to campers, too. Many behavioral incidents arise from too much unstructured time. When kids don't know what they're supposed to be doing, it affects emotional safety and paves the way for conflict. And everyone, from kids to counselors to leaders, will appreciate someone who invests the energy in helping them be a better member of the team. Good growth communication is a skill worth honing—it's why people's favorite teachers are also often their strictest, their favorite counselors are the ones who pushed them the most, and their most treasured friends are the ones who they tackled something new with. Growth is a bonding agent.

Regardless of whether communication will be your team's central triangle, it's also a worthwhile exercise to identify which arena of communication your team most needs to work on. Again, this doesn't mean the others fall by the wayside. But, like with the broader task of choosing a central triangle, the mere discussion of where your team could improve will a) elicit valuable feedback from many voices, and b) present a chance, in and of itself, to practice effective communication.

Intersection #C1: Communication x Focus → **Clarity**

Please refer to Intersection #F1 earlier in this section.

Intersection #C2: Communication x Accountability → **Transparency**

Please refer to Intersection #A2 earlier in this section.

Intersection #C3: Communication x Trust → **Authenticity**

Authenticity refers to being genuine, transparent and true to oneself in communication and interactions with others. It involves expressing thoughts, feelings and intentions honestly and sincerely, fostering trust and building strong relationships. This is mainly relevant to feedback (aka growth communication). As Maria says during the team dinner in Denver, members of an organization should be able to communicate real and respectful feedback to one another, while trusting that said feedback will be received well. An organization that cannot support the give and take of authentic feedback cannot succeed in its goals.

But authenticity is also related to team chemistry (aka relational communication). Maria, as a newcomer to Blue Trail, makes an effort to get to know every person on her staff, beyond just their role in the Blue Trail ecosystem. There should be room for genuine human interaction between supervisors and workers, and not just as a "warmup" to a work-related conversation. Offerings like the staff talent show contributed to the healthier, warmer culture at Blue Trail this summer. The leadership team carved out space during their staff training week for the staff to simply bond over each other's talents, with no professional considerations to speak of during that window of time. On a micro level, consider the relationship between Miguel and Nico. Despite their difference in professional roles, they had years of authentic friendship to lean on when Nico, as a supervisor, had to have a bit of an awkward conversation with Miguel about the story he shared during staff training. In a workplace that can boast true authenticity in relationships, tension and feedback are easier to navigate, because people are naturally more motivated to resolve issues with people they care about.

TRUST

"Teams that trust each other can accomplish anything they want. They set a clear goal and they trust each other to do what is necessary to accomplish it. They're open to feedback when they're getting a little off course, and most importantly, they feel empowered to give feedback to others on the team."

The least stressful workplaces are the ones that have the most investment in building trust. Employees don't need to be micromanaged, because supervisors trust that everyone is tackling their responsibilities with skill and professionalism. Supervisors are well-informed about items that may need a course correction, because employees trust that they won't be diminished for asking for help.

Trust is, again, something that is paramount specifically in camp environments. Camps are an opportunity to model an ideal workplace for young adults. We can choose to teach young people that it's okay to ask for help, that self-reflection and a growth mindset are desirable qualities in a team member. We can choose to teach young people that feedback is not a punishment. We can choose to engage with tension, rather than gossip. All of these things require, and promote, trust.

In the end, organizations create trust through members doing what they say they will do. From the smallest tasks to the broad-strokes missions, actions speak just as loud as words.

Maria and Samira spend a great deal of staff training talking about feedback, how they want it to flow freely between everyone on the staff and not just in response to catastrophic mistakes. Imagine if they had said all that and then reverted to Blue Trail's old habits, the ones that didn't promote growth. Imagine that they would have let the behaviors that Maria observed in week five slide. Nobody would have trusted Maria and Samira, because their words ("feedback isn't just for disasters!") wouldn't have matched their actions. Their behavior would have been something worse than apathy: hypocrisy.

Instead, throughout the summer, Maria and the rest of the leadership team practiced what they preached, including in their week five talk with the counselors. Take the exchange with Brandon, for example. He came into the week five meeting with nothing to report. There were no fights, no meltdowns, no emergency situations that he needed help triaging. But Maria and Samira trusted Brandon enough to know that he wouldn't perceive a little extra push as confrontational, so they asked him to dig deeper into the dynamics of his cabin. He did and it allowed him to grow as a counselor. Weeks of intentionally building trust, expressing clear values and taking actions that aligned with those values, paid off in this moment and many others.

Intersection #T1: Trust x Focus → **Alignment**

Please refer to Intersection #F3 earlier in this section.

Intersection #T2: Trust x Accountability → **Integrity**

Please refer to Intersection #A3 earlier in this section.

Intersection #T3: Trust x Communication → **Authenticity**

Please refer to Intersection #C3 earlier in this section.

*   *   *

The triangle model is not intended to be used in emergencies only. Due to the ability of the triangles to move in and out of the center, the model can and should be used in good times and hard times. The Blue Trail team, despite a successful summer, is already looking toward the next one and they end the fable agreeing that they need to shift their collective gaze toward improving communication. This isn't a defeat or a reduction of their good work over the course of the summer. It's simply an acknowledgement that tension will always exist within organizations.

High-performing teams, though, reflect often and anticipate issues, acknowledging that everyone, at all times, is growing. They are constantly reorienting themselves toward their shared focus; they take accountability and hold each other accountable; they communicate proactively and authentically; and they trust in the professionalism and good intentions of everyone on the team.

In our model, tension is not something to be avoided. It is indeed like a rubber band, something to be kept at the appropriate level of tautness to hold a team together. The band can snap or buckle, leaving the organization weakened. Thorough, active work on all four triangles, however, leads to an organization that can engage with tension, not as a side quest that distracts from accomplishing their goals, but in order to accomplish their goals. After all, there is no growth without tension.

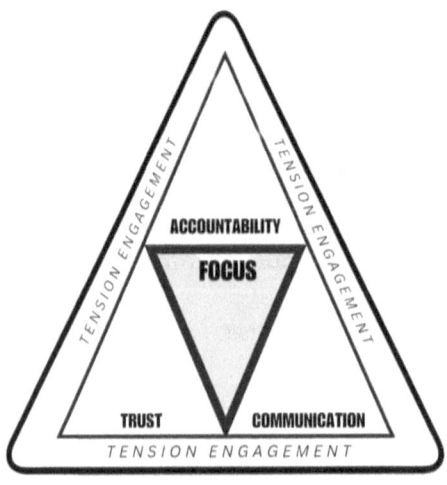

ACKNOWLEDGEMENTS

FROM BOB:

TO write a book many pieces need to fall in place, but two, in particular, hold the most importance. First, you have to have something to say that others will find of value. Second, you need to be able to say it in a way that others will find engaging.

After a half century of learning from others, I finally felt like I had something to say. And, after watching my oldest son turn himself into a writer with skills beyond what I could dream of, I had a way to share it so that people would enjoy and appreciate it.

So, the first acknowledgement should be to Ari, whose gifts have allowed us to accomplish a dream of mine. Thank you for both product and process. (And to his phenomenal agent, Seth, who would cry foul were he not to be mentioned with equal amounts of praise.)

I am also aware that if I have something worth sharing, it is only because of those who shared willingly of their time, patience, expertise and wisdom. I have had the rare honor of being able to name multiple people in my life who have acted as role models, mentors, and teachers. While Ari and I may be the scribes, it is their wisdom that sits at the heart of our work. Gratitude to each and every one who has been my teacher.

Finally, to those who have encouraged me to figure out what I want to do professionally and then supported my efforts to get there, I offer much appreciation. There are many people who fit this description; chief among them is my wife, Alexis, whose support is unwavering.

FROM ARI:

FIRST and foremost, I want to thank my dad for trusting me to put his thoughts onto the page. This whole project felt like a conversation with him, and conversations with him are always rich and warm. With each of his comments and suggested revisions, I learned something new. My own thoughts, young and untested, were tempered by his ample experience in so many arenas of leadership. His theory resonated so deeply with me that writing this book became as much of a pleasure and a learning experience as it was a challenge.

I owe an enormous debt of gratitude to all of my writing teachers, professors, and classmates at the University of San Francisco and The Willow School, whose endless talent and wisdom made me into the kind of person who would be asked to lend a hand to a project like this. Writing means being part of a community and I have been fortunate to be a part of some amazing spaces.

Our initial readers—trusted friends, family, and mentors—encountered these characters and this camp in its less-refined stages and gave us the kind of honest, belief-filled feedback Maria and co. would be proud of. It was never discouraging, but always incisive, and it always made me eager to come back to the page. Thank you all so very much.

BOB BERK, the founder and principal consultant of New Table Consulting, brings a wealth of knowledge and expertise to his work. With a focus on building capacity in individuals and organizations, Bob has a particular interest in the dynamics of high-performing teams, communication and conflict resolution.

Bob's passion lies in working with executives and employee teams across various sectors, tailoring his services to meet their unique needs. He excels in conflict resolution through mediation, facilitative dialogues, and restorative conversations. Additionally, he provides coaching for individuals and teams, specializing in leadership dyads. Bob also offers training services on a variety of topics, including trust, team effectiveness, feedback, and leadership development.

With an engaging and respectful style, Bob captivates audiences of all generations and seniority levels as a well-regarded presenter and speaker. As a former school principal with a passion for serving kids with special needs, Bob has a deep commitment for ensuring that each individual has an opportunity to be heard and make an impact on the communities in which they live and work.

Bob's academic credentials include a Bachelor's degree in Biology, a Master's degree in Secondary School Administration, and a PhD in Leadership and Policy. His diverse educational background contributes to his ability to approach leadership and team dynamics from multiple perspectives.

Bob's passion for camping is undeniable. With eleven summers spent as a camper, counselor, and CIT Director at Camp Timberlane for Boys in Northern Wisconsin, Bob credits camp for so much of what he has become, both personally and professionally. These experiences have profoundly shaped him, fostering meaningful relationships and imparting invaluable leadership lessons. Notably, Bob has had the privilege of continuing to work with camps at conferences and guiding camp staff during pre-camp in recent years.

ARI BERK is a Masters in Education student at the University of San Francisco, where he served as an editor of *Ignatian* literary magazine for two years. He has a passion for writing and workshopping prose of all kinds, and wants to share this energy with students of his own in the future. His essays and short stories have been honored with statewide and departmental prizes. He worked as a camp counselor for four summers in high school and college and attended sleepaway camp for three summers as a youth.

www.ingramcontent.com/pod-product-compliance
Lightning Source LLC
Chambersburg PA
CBHW030246130626
46549CB00002B/405